Dr Rev George Oliver 33°

1782 - 1867

Hand-Drawn Portrait by Jessica Naomi

George Oliver Masonic Writings

Dr Rev George Oliver 33°

Complied with Edits and Graphics by Darrell Jordan

Athenaia.Co

George Oliver Masonic Writings - Compiled with graphics and edits by
Darrell Jordan, Copyright © First Edition 2024. All rights reserved.
No part of this book may be reproduced in
whole or in part without the written
permission from the publisher, nor stored in any re-
trieval system or transmitted by
any means, electronic, mechanical, photocopy-
ing, recording, or other, without the
written consent of the publisher.
For bulk purchases, please contact the publisher.
Enquiry@Athenaia.Co
Library of Congress Cataloging-in Publication Data
Names: Oliver, George | Jordan, Darrell
Title: George Oliver Masonic Writings / Darrell Jordan, MPS
Description: First U.S. edition. | Coeur D'Alene, Idaho: Athenaia [2024]
Identifiers: LCCN (pending) |
ISBN 979-888556-051-1 (First Edition hardcover)
Subjects: OCC016000: BODY, MIND & SPIRIT / Occultism |
HI036000: PHILOSOPHY / Hermeneutics |
REL047000: RELIGION / Mysticism
LC record available at https://lccn. loc.gov

On the internet: Parallel47North.com/collections/esoteric-books
Managing Editor: Darrell Jordan
Original Author and Essay: George Oliver
Executive Producer: Yuka Jordan
Book Cover Design by Yuka Jordan
Book Cover Art and Illustrations: Jessica Naomi
Image Credits: George Oliver's and Darrell Jordan's personal collection
Printed and bound in the United States

Publisher: Athenaia, LLC
2370 N Merritt Crk Lp, Ste 1
Coeur D'Alene, ID 83814
The United States

Dedication

*To those who Search for Truth and
a Path with Heart.*

Contents

Forward by William Dixson, P.M.

FORWARD 13

ADDITIONAL INFORMATION 37

Masonic Writings
George Oliver

THE NUMBER THREE 39

EVIDENCES, DOCTRINES, AND TRADITIONS 75

INFLUENCE ON THE MORAL AND SOCIAL CONDITION OF MAN 87

THE EMBLEMATICAL REFERENCES OF THE SUN IN A MASONIC LODGE 121

ON THE OBJECTIONS OF SOME OF THE ANGLO-INDIAN CLERGY 135

ON THE LANDMARKS OF MASONRY 145

THE GREAT PLAN OF HUMAN SALVATION TRACED IN FREE-MASONRY 161

ON FREEMASONRY 171

"Masonic Offering" to the Rev. George Oliver, D.D.

MASONIC OFFERING TO THE REV. GEO. OLIVER, D.D. ... 185

Author and Managing Eitor
Darrell Jordan

About the Managing Editor 193

Books By The Managing Editor 195

Artist and Illustrator
Jessica Naomi

Hand-Drawn Portrait of George Oliver 197

Other Illustrations & Portraits by the Artist 199

Forward by William Dixson, P.M.

With Additional Information about George Oliver

FORWARD

Few, if any, writers on Speculative Masonry, have been more popular amongst the craft than the Rev. Dr. George Oliver. This excellent man and eminent Mason was born at Papplewick, near Nottingham, the parochial register recording the baptism of George, son of Samuel and Elizabeth Oliver, on November 9th, 1782.

Little is recorded of George Oliver's early days beyond that he attended the Grammar School at Nottingham. This would probably be during the time his father resided at Gotham.

As already noted in the memoir of the Rev. Samuel Oliver, the family moved to Whaplode in the latter part of 1801.

Soon after this, George Oliver was initiated as a Lewis in the St. Peter's Lodge, Peterborough, Brother Stephens being then W.M. It is somewhat remarkable that the precise date of the initiation has never been satisfactorily settled. The following is transcribed from the Grand Secretary's Letter Book:

"Freemasons Hall 3rd Aug. 1819.

"Brother, The Rev. George Oliver, who was initiated in your lodge about the year 1802-1803 having applied for a Grand Lodge Certificate, it has been found upon examining the Books of the Grand Lodge that his name has never been returned for registry by your lodge; this neglect on your part has been communicated to the Board of General Purposes, and we are directed by that Board to require, that you will immediately register the Name of that

Brother, and of any other which may have been neglected to be transmitted for that purpose."

We are, &c. "Master of 605 St. Peters Peterborough."

What answer was returned to this request is not known, but apparently the matter was never cleared up. Among the Doctor's MSS., now in possession of Prov. G. Lodge, is a draft of a speech delivered about 1842 relating to his Masonic career. It begins, "When I was first initiated into Masonry, in I think 1801, I resided more than 20 miles from a Lodge."

From this expression it is evident that nothing fixing the date had come to hand.

The account of the proceedings of the St. Peter's brethren, both in ordinary meetings and initiations, as furnished in the Doctor's speech, is extremely interesting, and one is not surprised to find the Secretary occasionally omitting to register all their doings. About 1803 George Oliver was appointed Usher or Assistant Master of the Grammar School at Castor, Lincolnshire, and on April 15th, 1805, he married Miss Mary Ann Beverley, of an old Caistor family dating back many years. According to the Doctor's reminiscences, no Masonic connection was kept up during the time he was at Caistor. On May 30th, 1809, Bro. Oliver was elected Head Master of the Grammar School at Great Grimsby, and very soon set about forming a Masonic Lodge. In 1811 Grand Lodge was notified that the Warrant No. 510, granted in 1792 to constitute the Urania Lodge at Brigg, afterwards removed to Louth, was established at Grimsby under the name of Apollo. In the following year, the foundation stone of a Masonic Hall was laid; the Lodge entered upon a very flourishing career, and its Master upon that study of the craft which has rendered his name famous.

An extract from one of the Doctor's later works tells us how absorbing at this time his thoughts and ideas of Masonry became, and it may well be taken as the keynote of those remarkable works which afterwards came so readily from his pen:

"It was a noble Lodge Room appropriated to the sole purpose of Masonry. I had a private key, and many an hour have I spent in solitary enjoyment, when no one knew the building contained an inmate. Here my first aspirations to contribute to the benefit of the Order were imbibed.

Here vast projects were formed, with none present but my Almighty Father and myself which have not yet been developed. Here surrounded by the Implements of Masonry, I became impressed with sublime ideas of its superlative blessedness, and universal application to science and morals, and determined to work out principles which were then so feebly scattered as to give rise, amongst the uninitiated, to fantastic notions and absurd opinions respecting the design and end of the Institution, that derogated from the virtue and holiness of this sacred handmaid of religion."

Brother Oliver appears to have been acquainted not only with the degrees of Freemasonry recognized at the present day, but with others now obsolete. Several of the degrees were taken in Hull, where he was highly esteemed, and where recollections of his genial disposition and excellent company yet linger among the brethren of the Minerva Lodge. In 1845, Dr. Oliver was one of the original members of the Supreme Council 33 Degree of England and Wales.

In the early part of the century, some of these degrees were conferred "according to merit and ability" in the ordinary Lodge. No instance of such, however, appears in the Lincolnshire records except the Mark degree in the Witham. The P.G. Master's instructions to his Deputy (as seen in the life of the Rev. M. Barnett) on this subject probably discouraged the practice. In 1813-1 5 George Oliver was ordained in the Church of England, and became Curate of Grimsby, under Dr. Tennyson, and Vicar of Clee on the presentation of the Bishop of Lincoln (Tomline).

The preferment which Oliver afterwards obtained, has occasioned his biographers, almost without exception, under the erroneous idea that he simultaneously held all his livings, to lay him open to a charge of being a pluralist.

The following extracts from the Episcopal Records show this imputation to be only partially correct, the reverend gentleman apparently never holding more than two livings together, the joint net income from which only realizing a modest amount:

George Oliver instituted to the Vicarage of Clee 11th July, 1815. His successor was instituted in 1835.

George Oliver instituted to the Vicarage of Scopwick 12th Oct, 1831; his successor in 1867.

(Patron, Bishop Kaye).

George Oliver was appointed to the Collegiate Church of Wolverhampton (a Royal Peculiar) in 1834. Patron, Dean of Windsor. His successor in 1847.

George Oliver instituted to the Rectory of South Hykeham 17th May, 1847 (exchange); his successor in 1867.

These appointments scarcely justify the expression used by one of his biographers, that "Oliver was a fine specimen of the Pluralist system." The duties appertaining to the ministry were always conscientiously performed and gained for him the esteem and respect of his parishioners.

The following bespeaks the Man, the Mason, and the Christian Minister:

At a vestry meeting held on 27th April, 1840, at Wolverhampton, to appoint Churchwardens for the ensuing year, the Rev. George Oliver, the Incumbent, addressed the parishioners on the subject of Church Rates:

"As to the legality of Church Rates," said the reverend gentlemen, "I continue to hold the sentiments I have heretofore professed; but when I consider that the granting of such rates is optional, and that the discussion of the subject only tends to create feud, to divide the town against itself to set father against son, and son against father—to sever long-standing friendships, and to dissolve mutual ties; when I reflect also that the agitation of that question is little less than a scourge on the public peace of the town, I cannot consent to aim a blow so heavy and a discouragement so great on what I consider to be the interests of the Church.

I shall not give my consent, therefore, to the agitation of the question of the Church Rates. My motto is 'Peace,' and the banner I unfurl this day is the banner of Unity—a banner which cannot, as it shall not, be raised to lead you into contests in which all is to be lost and nothing is to be gained.

"I know I shall be asked how I purpose, without a rate to provide for the congregational expenses of the Church? My answer is simple. I have no doubt whatever of the success of the voluntary system if it is properly tested. I shall, with the assistance of my warden and the colleague you may appoint to act with him, give this plan a fair and free trial; and so long as I continue the resident incumbent of this parish, I pledge myself never to go for a rate if you will support me, which I repeat, I have no doubt you will, in defraying the congregational expenses of the Church by your voluntary contributions."

Sentiments like these were by no means common fifty years ago; they show the character of the Doctor, and account in a great measure for the grief and indignation which was shown when one of the great sorrows of his life occurred—his removal from the office of D.P.G.M. Had not this event so greatly affected our Province, one would willingly have omitted so discreditable a chapter in Masonic history.

One of the most active and energetic of the London brethren was R. T. Crucifix, M.D., editor and proprietor of the Freemason Quarterly Review, and who was a personal friend of Dr. Oliver. About the year 1834 Brother Crucifix, in conjunction with others, suggested in the columns of his Review the establishment of a third Grand Charity, "An Asylum for Aged and Decayed Freemasons."

The idea appeared to be warmly taken up both in London and

the Provinces, and for a time everything went smoothly.

But owing to some cause or other the proposal was coldly looked upon by an influential portion of the craft, including the Duke of Sussex (Grand Master), C. T. D'Eyncourt (Prov. G. Master for Lincolnshire), and many others who, while not showing direct opposition, yet treated the scheme in a half-hearted manner. The project dragged along till the close of 1839, the breach between the parties gradually becoming wider.

On Nov. 13th, a meeting of the governors of the Institution was held, Dr. Crucifix being in the chair. During the meeting it was alleged that two brethren, T. Wood and J. L. Stevens, had spoken disrespectfully of H.R.H. the Grand Master, and they were accordingly summoned before the Board of General Purposes to answer the charge, Dr. Crucifix, as Chairman of the meeting, being also summoned for not checking the speakers.

After a very one-sided trial, the three were suspended for a time from their Masonic privileges, the following:

Grand Lodge dismissing their appeal and confirming the sentence. Crucifix, naturally indignant at the way these proceedings had been carried on, immediately took steps to sever his connection with the craft. The Lodges of which he was a member, viz., the Lodge of Concord, the Burlington, and the Bank of England Lodges, received his resignation with expressions of the deepest and most sincere regret, the latter placing on its minutes "That this Lodge desires further to record the expression of its extreme sorrow and indignation at the events which have produced a result so deeply to be deplored."

At the same time Crucifix addressed a very intemperate letter to the Grand Master, announcing his withdrawal from the craft, and charging the Duke with having been unmindful of his obl., as regards the Ancient Charges, also that on one occasion his language had been such "as was calculated to lower the respect due to the person of your Royal Highness and above all, to the dignified office of Grand Master."

There can be no question that this letter was ill-advised, especially as the writer was simply suspended, and merited from Grand Lodge the severest condemnation.

At an Especial Grand Lodge held 30th October, 1840, the case was gone into, and Bro. Crucifix tendered an apology.

Amongst the speakers who supported a motion for Crucifix being expelled, i.e., "that the apology be not accepted," was the Rt. Hon. C. T. D'Eyncourt, P.G.M. for Lincolnshire.

On a division being taken, 127 were for expulsion and 145 against. As to the right and wrong in these proceedings, one thing is very evident—both sides lost their temper and their dignity. There is no doubt H.R.H. the Grand Master fully appreciated his high position, and felt no misgivings as to his ability and fitness in carrying out the attributes of K.S. and H.K.T.; and it must be acknowledged that the craft attained much dignity and honor among the popular world at large during his long term of office. As to Crucifix, though unpleasant rumors were in circulation as to his early life, the numerous letters received by Oliver, now in our P.G.L. Library, testify to the high character of the writer. He was an energetic worker in the cause of excellent business habits, and a writer of considerable merit. A great number of aged brethren and their widows have had reason to bless the day that Robert Thomas Crucifix saw the light of Masonry, and the Freemason Quarterly Review for its persistent advocacy of what is now the third Central Charity of English Masonry, the Royal Masonic Institution for Aged Freemasons.

The publication in the Review of the proceedings in Grand Lodge, was strongly disapproved of by a large portion of the craft, as being both illegal and inexpedient, and it is pretty evident that the opposition to the Asylum scheme, partook more of ill-will to the Journal and its Editor, than to the charity itself In order to see how these events effected our own Prov. G. Lodge it will be necessary to turn back a little.

From the first suggestion of the new charity, Doctor Oliver, as would naturally be expected, gave it his heartiest good wishes and support. In his capacity as D.P.G.M. he sent to the various Lodges a circular-letter of several pages, not only advocating the cause as a Masonic principle, but giving a practical instance of its necessity.

At the P.G.L. held at Grantham in 1839, Crucifix was invited to attend and explain the principles on which the Asylum was founded. And throughout the whole of the proceedings in Grand Lodge, Oliver's sympathy and assistance were always with his friend to cheer and support him in his efforts. How these were appreciated is shown by the following quotation from the Review:

"I must assure him (Dr. Oliver) that, however, I have been cheered and inspirited under most eventful and trying circumstances, by the sympathy of the kind, the generous, and the free; I have been mainly sustained by endeavors to observe his directions—to rely with reverence and humility on the justice of a merciful Providence."

Towards the end of 1839, a movement was set on foot to present Dr. Crucifix with a testimonial. A strong committee was formed, with Bro. J. Lee Stevens, of the Bank of England Lodge, as Secretary. Notwithstanding that individual subscriptions were limited to 10s, the fund rapidly amounted to £250, and the festival was fixed for 24th November, 1841, the presentation to be made by the Very Worshipful Brother, the Rev. Dr. Oliver, "Unapproachable in Masonic lore—inimitable as a Masonic writer—unequaled in the performance of Masonic rites and the practice of Masonic virtues—at once our oracle and historian, our model and our guide—to whom, but to him, should be confided this labor of love?" The announcement was received with general satisfaction by the subscribers, to most of whom Oliver was personally a stranger, and they hailed with delight the prospect of seeing and hearing one who, besides being the intimate friend of Crucifix, was by far the ablest writer on the staff of the Review.

The proceedings were held under the auspices of the Bank of England Lodge, the following summons being sent to members and subscribers:

"Crucifix Testimonial Festival." Bank of England Lodge No. 329 New London Hotel Bridge St. Bro. J. Lee Stevens W.M.

"Sir & Bro.," 17 Nov. 1841.

"You are requested to attend the duties of the Lodge on Wednesday next the 24th inst. at 3 for 4 o'clock in the afternoon punctually. Dinner on table at Six o'clock. Subscribers to the Crucifix Testimonial & Festival are invited to visit the Lodge at 4 o'clock."

Scarcely a member was absent on the occasion. As soon as the brethren were arranged in their places, the Lodge was opened, and the Rev. G. Oliver, D.D., was unanimously elected an honorary member, pursuant to notice previously given.

The Master then gracefully requested the Doctor to accept the chair and preside for the remainder of the evening, a request that was immediately complied with, and the "Philosopher of Masonry" presided for the first time in London, over the largest meeting of Masons ever assembled in a private Lodge.

A portion of the First Lecture was worked by brethren of the Emulation Lodge, and the Doctor delivered an oration founded on the Fifth Ancient Charge.

Dr. Oliver, according to arrangement, afterwards took the chair at the banquet, having Dr. Crucifix on his right and J. Lee Stevens on his left. The usual Loyal and Masonic Toasts were admirably proposed, the toast of the evening, the health of Dr. Crucifix, being given in such a manner as to add to the Doctor's already high reputation! The evident sincerity of his praise, his sympathy with Crucifix in his late trials, and the flattering testimony he bore to the value of the Review, placing him in full accord with his audience.

At the close of his speech the Doctor, according to Lincolnshire custom, led off with the firing, a proceeding apparently novel at that time to the London brethren, but which pleased them intensely, and resumed his seat amidst the most enthusiastic applause.

The festival was a great success, and although it could not be otherwise but that some reference would be made to the recent proceedings in Grand Lodge, the matters were touched upon in such a manner as to convey no personal allusion.

It should be noted that subsequent to the proposition for the expulsion of Dr. Crucifix, moved, as already stated, by the P.G. Master for Lincolnshire, and also after the arrangements had been made for the Crucifix presentation, Dr. Oliver, doubtless actuated by a nice sense of honor and a desire of promoting the best interests of the craft, tendered his resignation as D.P.G.M.

The P.G.M. at the Boston meeting announced the tendered resignation, declaring his refusal to accept it, and making an urgent request to the Doctor to continue in his office. This was on 29th Sept, 1841. Early in the following spring, the Witham brethren proceeded to make arrangements for consecrating their new hall, and the Doctor wrote to the P.G.M. to know his wishes on the subject, receiving, doubtless much to his amazement, the following answer:

"5 Albemarle St.

"4th Mar. 1842.

"My dear Sir,

"I was at Gloucester when yours of the 28th reached London. I confess I feel uncomfortable on the subject of it. I do not know at this distance of time, whether I can attend, and if I do not, you would have to officiate for me. Now, it will probably have occurred to you, that I am placed in a very painful situation in consequence of your having presided at the dinner given to Dr. Crucifix. I have not seen the Duke of Sussex, and have avoided waiting upon him, because I think when I do so, I may have to deal with the subject, but I cannot postpone my visit beyond a few days. I know from private sources that His Royal Highness has expressed a very strong opinion in regard to your presiding on the occasion I have referred to; and if you were now to be seen on a great public occasion officiating as my deputy, he might consider me a party.

I came up to town above a year ago, when the case of Dr. Crucifix was before Grand Lodge in order to be present at the hearing, and took a prominent part myself in the course of it. "Under these circumstances, it may be better to postpone any reply to the Witham Lodge until it can be seen whether I can attend.

"I am my dear Sir

"Yours truly

"C. T. D'Eyncourt."

The Witham brethren, having received no answer to their request, again wrote to the Doctor. He forwarded the letter to the Prov. G. Master, and received the following reply:

"Bayons Manor Market Rasen

"28 April 1842.

"Dear Sir & Brother,

"You are aware of the circumstances which have influenced my judgment when I feel myself called upon now to declare vacant the office of Deputy Provincial Grand Master for Lincolnshire, held by you. In communicating this my determination to you I beg to express my best acknowledgements for the service you have rendered the Masonic body within my jurisdiction during the time you have held the office, and my regret that the interests of Masonry should require me to deprive myself of your valuable assistance.

"The separation gives me, personally, as much pain as the cause of it; and none the less because my decision is one which I have thought it right to make on my own responsibility, without reference to or suggestion from any other party.

"I am dear Sir

"Yours fraternally

"Charles Tennyson D'Eyncourt

"Rev. George Oliver D.D." "P.G.M. Lincolnshire.

The Doctor on receipt of this letter communicated at once with the various Lodges in the Province. The Witham brethren, at a Lodge of Emergency, passed a strong resolution on the subject, copies of which were forwarded both to the P.G.M. and his late deputy.

This was acknowledged by the Doctor as follows:

"Scopwick Vicarage

"June 7th, 1842.

"My dear Sir & Bro.

"I beg to acknowledge the receipt of a resolution passed in the Witham Lodge on the 2nd of May last, and beg them brethren will accept my cordial thanks for the kind expression of their sentiments on my dismissal from the office of Deputy Prov. G. Master for Lincolnshire.

"As I am not conscious of having violated any masonic law, or neglected the performance of any masonic duty in the above capacity, my conscience acquits me of any willful disrespect to the authority of the P.G.M. It is true I have assisted at the formation of a Fund of Benevolence for the relief of worthy aged & decayed Freemasons, and I have been an instrument in the hands of the craft to reward the philanthropist who originated that beneficent plan.

"If these be crimes to call forth public indignation, then is my punishment just. But if on the contrary. Benevolence be a masonic virtue, then I must consider my dismissal to be undeserved.

"Believe me, Dear Sir,

"Your faithful Brother,

"Geo. Oliver,

"Past D.P.G.M. for Lincolnshire.

FORWARD

"The W.M. & Brethren of the Witham Lodge."

Two days after the date of this communication, the Witham brethren met to dedicate their new Hall in Saltergate. The P.G.M. having declined to fulfil his promise of summoning a Provincial Lodge, the ceremony was performed by the W.M. of the Witham, Bro. Robert Goodacre, assisted by Bro. E. A. Bromehead as D.C. and Bro. W. A. Nicholson, the Architect of the building. Dr. Oliver, in his capacity as Chaplain of the Lodge, taking the consecrating portion.

The proceedings appear to have been planned and carried out very effectively. Bro. Edw. Dearie, Mus. Bac, Cantab, (at that time a somewhat rare degree), directed the musical portion of the ceremony, two of the hymns being written respectively by the W.M. and D.C.

There was a large attendance of brethren, due in some measure to the notice that the Lodge would celebrate its centenary (how this was calculated is not recorded), but principally, no doubt, to hear what the Doctor had to say regarding his dismissal, it being his first public appearance since the event. In this, they were not disappointed. The Doctor, in acknowledging the toast of his health, read the letters received from the P.G.M., and made a very lengthy and telling speech, embracing the Constitutions, Provincial By-laws, and the leading Masonic virtues, summing up the matter as follows:

"I was the instrument through whom the craft presented a testimonial to Dr. Crucifix, because he is a benevolent man, and has succeeded by a great sacrifice both of time and money in establishing a noble Institution. The P.G.M. proposed in Grand Lodge that this man to whom the craft is under such weighty obligations should be expelled. Now, brethren, which do you think is to be most commended? I who was an instrument in rewarding virtue, or the P.G.M. who would have punished it. I can conscientiously say that I have not sought popularity by illegitimate means I have never endeavored to make a party by the sacrifice of masonic principles. I have, on all occasions, discharged my duty without fear, favor, or partiality."

The following extract from the current number of the Lincolnshire Chronicle exhibited not only the opinions of the local brethren, but also of many others who saw in the recent proceedings of Grand Lodge the only key to the extraordinary action of the P.G.M.:

"The only assignable motive which could have actuated the P.G.M. in this extraordinary step, after the repeated declarations he has made of how greatly he is indebted to Dr. Oliver for his aid in conducting the masonic affairs of the Province is, that he has been prompted by some high power to make the attack."

"The character of Dr. Oliver as a freemason, even with those who are inimical to the craft, is too high to need any eulogy on our part; the only intelligible motive is, that there is a determination on the part of those behind the masonic throne, to discountenance and even to punish any who shall dare to promote a charity which is not yet recognized by the laws of the craft; and Dr. Oliver, who has been justly termed the 'Sage of Masonry', has been selected as an illustrious example to prove that such determination will be carried out with no feeble or tardy spirit."

At the close of the Lincoln meeting, a Committee was appointed to take the necessary steps for presenting the Doctor with a General Masonic Testimonial. Accordingly, a meeting was held on Thursday, 11th August, 1842, the Mayor of Lincoln (Bro. George Wriglesworth Hebb) in the chair, being supported by Bro. W. H. Adams (Mayor of Boston), Bro. Richd. Sutton Harvey, and representatives from most of the Lodges in the Province, a Sub-Committee being also formed in London to work with the Lincoln brethren, of which the very energetic Bro. J. Lee Stevens was Secretary.

There appears to have been an understanding that the various resolutions submitted should contain no allusion to the recent dismissal, and that the speakers should, if possible, avoid any irritating reference. Doubtless this was wise counsel, and the proper course to pursue, as it allowed both sides to take part, and above all, enabled the P.G.M. to show his appreciation of his late deputy's services without loss of dignity, and thus pave the way for a reconciliation.

It was a most critical period for the craft in Lincolnshire, and the next Provincial meeting, which had been fixed to be held at Spalding, was looked forward to with great anxiety and apprehension. The publicity given in the local papers, the well-known character and ability of Oliver, his personal friendship with all the working Masons in the Province on the one side, against the evident unpopularity of the P.G.M., marked a serious state of affairs.

On 29th September the Rt. Hon. C. T. D'Eyncourt, Prov. G. Master, attended by his new deputy, the Rev. Geo. Coltman, Rector of Stickney, opened Prov. G. Lodge at Spalding.

The Rev. Dr. Oliver, P.D.P.G.M., supported by his friends, Dr. Crucifix and J. L. Stevens, who had come down specially to attend a testimonial meeting, the Doctor's father, the Rev. S. Oliver (then in his ninetieth year), and the Doctor's son—three generations—being also present.

After the usual routine business, the brethren proceeded in procession to Church, the sermon being preached by the Rev. W. Muckler from Ps. cxxxiii., "Behold, how good and joyful a thing it is, brethren, to dwell together in unity."

Mr. Muckler's name does not appear on the Provincial roll. Whether he was merely the deputy of the P.G. Chaplain, the Rev. G. Coltman, who under the peculiar circumstances, could not very well occupy the pulpit, or whether he was specially selected to recall the brethren to a sense of their mutual obligation, is not known; but it may be truthfully said, that of the numberless times this masonic text had been preached from, there never was an occasion which presented a better opportunity for the preacher's eloquence, than this assembly of Lincolnshire Masons in Spalding Church on the Feast of St. Michael and All Angels, 1842. On the Lodge resuming at two o'clock, the P.G.M. entered into an elaborate review of the recent events, in the course of which there appeared, he said, to have been some misunderstanding.

The address, which lasted two hours, would doubtless show the eminent abilities of the speaker to the best advantage.

Dr. Oliver replied, and the debate was continued by Bros. J. L. Stevens and W. H. Adams. The Doctor's speech, a draft of which is among his MSS., now in possession of P.G.L., was a most impassioned appeal for justice, and one may easily imagine its effect upon the brethren.

From the meagre accounts to be found of the meeting, it appears that after mutual explanations had been entered into, a better spirit prevailed, which was cemented by the P.G.M. allowing the following resolution to be put:

"That this Provincial Grand Lodge entertains the warmest feelings of gratitude towards the Rev. George Oliver D.D. late D.P.G.M. for Lincolnshire, for his unwearied and successful efforts to promote the best interest of Free-masonry in general and in this Province in particular, & for the unequaled talent, research & industry displayed by him as a Masonic writer. That being duly impressed with a sense of his great public, private & social virtues, this P.G.L. cannot but deeply lament the loss of the very valuable services of Bro. Oliver as D.P.G.M., the duties of which office he for many years discharged so as to gain the veneration and esteem of the brethren generally and to call forth repeated marks of approbation from the P.G.M. That the sum of Five Guineas be paid from the funds of this P.G.L. in aid of the subscription now raising for the purpose of presenting to Bro. Oliver a Masonic offering as a mark of fraternal regard & of grateful acknowledgment of his invaluable services in the cause of Masonry."

The proceedings, so far, point to a more harmonious feeling

existing between the friends of the P.G.M. and those of his late Deputy; but one is scarcely prepared for such an exhibition of true Masonic spirit as was witnessed at the banquet which followed the Lodge. Could anyone who has followed these proceedings, or could any Brother who attended at Spalding on that memorable day have imagined that the dread and gloom which ushered in the meeting would be dispelled, and the force of the preacher's text "Behold how good and joyful for brethren to be in unity" be exemplified in such a forcible manner as probably had never been experienced by those hundred brethren who had the good fortune to be present?

And moreover, that the health of the P.G.M. should be proposed by Dr. Crucifix, the man whose expulsion from the craft had been moved in Grand Lodge by Brother D'Eyncourt; that the P.G.M. in returning thanks should say, "that he (Crucifix) had repaid unkindness by charity, and a too hasty judgment by the most benevolent construction of human error." Yet all this took place. Brother D'Eyncourt offered the right hand of fellowship to Brother Oliver; the worthy Doctor returned the greeting, comparing "the present gratifying re-union to nothing more opposite than the birth of Light. Freemasonry (said the Doctor) like the Sun in its refulgent brightness shed its glorious lustre over the plains of Lincolnshire, diffusing blessings wherever its light was displayed. Suddenly, its brightness was obscured by a dense and threatening cloud. This symbol of evil was the harbinger of terror and alarm. The struggle between light and darkness was short and transient— the holy principles of Freemasonry prevailed—the heavy cloud was dissipated. The Sun, emblem of Wisdom, Strength and Beauty burst forth in all its splendor, and when the Brethren were called from labor to refreshment, the brilliant prospect was renewed & the triumphant dominion of Light now promises to be permanent and enduring." In closing the account of this very unfortunate dispute, it is only fair to note that the Provincial G. Master was placed in a very difficult position.

For some years prior to the Crucifix proceedings in Grand

Lodge, Mr. D'Eyncourt had filled the post of Equerry to the Duke of Sussex, and very intimate relations were understood to subsist between them. The annoyance felt by the Grand Master with the contributors of the Review, would be considerably increased by the action of Bro. J. L. Stevens at the December Lodge, held to nominate the Grand Master for the ensuing year, when Bro. Stevens objected to the Duke's nomination and proposed the Marquis of Salisbury. This nobleman, of course, refused to stand, but the proceedings must nevertheless have been very disagreeable.

The intimacy between H.R.H. and Mr. D'Eyncourt accounts for the apparently anomalous action of the latter in Grand Lodge, for anomalous it certainly was, when measured by his well-known political principles.

The relation of the Crucifix party with the old members of Grand Lodge, may be likened in some measure to the two great political parties of the day. The views advocated by Crucifix in the Freemasons Quarterly Review were not unreasonable, and it is certainly remarkable that the "Radical Member for Lambeth" should move the expulsion of one, who was looked upon by a section of Grand Lodge in the same light, as the hon. member himself was by the opposite party in politics.

Amongst other things commented upon in the columns of the Review, was the lack of interest apparently shown by many Provincial Grand Masters in not summoning their annual Lodges. That the complaint was well grounded could not be denied, and though Lincolnshire was not so flagrant a case as some of its neighbors, the arrow evidently struck. The Witham brethren appear to have memorialized the P.G.M. on the subject, for in a speech at Lincoln on the occasion of laying the foundation stone of their new hall, Bro. D'Eyncourt says:

"The brethren at Lincoln were quite right in the respectful remonstrance which they had forwarded to him, in saying 'that according to the laws of Masonry the Provincial meetings ought to be held every year,' but," reasoned the speaker, "that was rather recommendatory than compulsory."

The Review in its criticism says:

"Whatever may be the literal construction of the law, whether it be recommendatory or compulsory, there cannot be a difference of opinion as to its spirit—its true intent and meaning. It may be very easy for those who sit in judgment in their own case, either in Lincoln or in London, to construe the law in their own favor. This is part of their peculiar privilege; but neither common sense nor masonic justice will be thus hoodwinked."

These were unpleasant remarks from a paper which numbered Dr. Oliver amongst its principal supporters. "Many mickles make a muckle," and doubtless they would weigh in the adverse balance with the Doctor's eminent services.

The testimonial, or as it was styled "Masonic Offering to Dr. Oliver," to which reference has already been made, was presented on 8th May, 1844. A banquet, towards which Bro. Colonel Sibthorp contributed venison, was held at Bro. Melton's, The City Arms. Owing to the lamented decease of Bro. G. W. Hebb, the duties of the chair devolved upon Bro. the Rev. J. O. Dakeyne, W.M. of the Witham Lodge.

The "Offering," which consisted of a silver cup together with a portion of silver destined for each of the Doctor's children, was borne into the room by four Past Masters, W. H. Adams, 339 Boston; W. A. Nicholson, 374 Lincoln; J. W. Pashley, 611 Gainsborough; and Z. Barton, 612 Market Rasen; preceded by Bro. R, Goodacre, 374, as Director of Ceremonies.

The presentation cup, in addition to the usual engraved heraldic and Masonic devices, bore an inscription written in Latin by Bro. Dakeyne, the following being a translation:

To George Oliver,
Doctor in Divinity and
Fellow of the Society of Antiquaries Edinburgh,
Vicar of Scopwick, Incumbent of Wolverhampton,

Lately in the County of Lincoln
Of Freemasons
Deputy Grand Master,
Also of the Witham Lodge 374 A Member and Chaplain,
A Philosopher & Archaeologian
Second to none. In Historical subjects most learned. An Orator
whether in Church or in our Councils,
Both in Knowledge and in Eloquence most excellent,
Of the Mystic Union
Founded in Brotherly love and truth
For 40 years the most Erudite Expositor,
A Brother of Reverence unceasingly most worthy,
The Brethren throughout the whole surface of the Earth
Celebrating the Rites of Freemasonry
For the sake both of Honour and love
Have given this A.D. 1844. Offering, A.L. 5844.

It may now be as well to glance at the clerical life of Bro. Oliver. One might almost fear from the absorbing devotion paid to Masonry, that the duties appertaining to the ministry would be neglected: happily such is not the case; the parochial records of Grimsby, Wolverhampton, and Scopwick, all pointing to an exemplary discharge of the office. Scopwick, at the time Mr. Oliver was appointed in 1831, was in such a state as to be a proverb and a by-word amongst the neighboring villages. No schools nor schoolroom; the church walls and floor covered with green moss, from which drops of water trickled continuously; scarcely any congregation; the churchyard wall in a ruinous condition; and the vicarage house and premises uninhabitable.

All these were remedied in a few years. A new vicarage built at the expense of the Vicar; the church made fit for service; a new school-room built, and a regular attendance of children both on Sunday and week-day.

In 1855 the Doctor decided to relinquish the personal supervision of his parish, a resolve made five years previously, but then withdrawn at the earnest desire of his parishioners.

He preached his farewell sermon on March 25th, 1855, in the course of which he said:

"I have been preaching the Gospel to you, my Brethren faithfully and sincerely these many years, until my physical powers are exhausted; and as I cannot continue to discharge the duties of the Church with satisfaction to myself or benefit to you, I reverentially conclude that it is the will of my Divine Master that I should no longer abide with you."

The rest of the Doctor's life was passed in Nottingham and Lincoln, his son, Beverley Oliver, being in business as a bookseller in the former town.

His first residence in Lincoln was Norman Place, here Mrs. Oliver died in 1856. For several years prior to his death, the Doctor resided in Eastgate in the house nearly opposite James Street, Mrs. Pears, a widowed daughter, living with him.

Though not taking any active part in the Province during the administration of the Earl of Yarborough, the late Deputy still took a lively interest in the proceedings of P.G.L.

On the appointment of the Duke of St. Albans, in 1863, he presided at the installation, and at the next meeting at Lincoln, May 10th, 1866, he delivered his farewell address to Prov. G. Lodge.

On Sunday evening, March 3rd, 1867, after an illness of about nine days, the venerable brother departed this life, his last act of earthly business being to send a donation to the new Provincial Benevolent Fund. The funeral took place on the following Thursday in the cemetery belonging to the parish of St. Swithin. The brethren of the Witham Lodge attended, and a portion of the Prestonian Ritual was observed under the direction of Bro. Charles Harrison, the W. Master. The burial ground is now in the midst of a thickly populated district, and was until recently about as desolate a spot as can be imagined. A modest monumental slate stone near the south-west corner marks the last resting place of this excellent man and renowned Freemason. One looks in vain for any sign on the stone indicating the grave of a Mason; not even a solitary square and compass appears to distinguish the grave from others around.

The following inscription is on either side:

> "In memory of
> The Rev. George Oliver D.D.
> who died the 3rd of March 1867
> In the 85th year of his age."
>
> ―
>
> "In memory of
> Mary Ann, Wife of the Rev. George Oliver D.D.
> who died the 13th of October 1856
> in the 80th year of her age."

Doctor Oliver is yet well remembered in Lincoln. All agree in their testimony to his good qualities. Nothing has (so far as is known) ever been laid to his charge, unworthy of a Mason or unbecoming a Clergyman. In business matters straightforward, charitable according to the limited means at his disposal; of a genial disposition, at the refreshment board, would sing a good song, enjoy a good joke, and was excellent company; but no whisper was ever heard that he exceeded the bounds of moderation. Many years ago, when hard drinking was the fashion, writing on what is now a popular degree in the craft, he says, "it is to be commended as containing an excellent charge on the beastly habit of drunkenness."

In the latter part of 1865, a movement was set on foot to gather subscriptions to aid the Doctor's somewhat slender resources. Bro. W. G. Moore, of the Witham Lodge, had the matter in hand, and a considerable amount was raised. After the Doctor's death, it was decided to employ the money in founding an Oliver Memorial. Various schemes were proposed, and ultimately it was decided to raise the amount up to one thousand guineas, and devote the interest towards the education of necessitous boys of the Province.

The idea was warmly taken up, and the Oliver Memorial Fund now perpetuates the memory of our late D.P.G.M. in a manner doubtless he himself would have desired. As a writer on Speculative Masonry Dr. Oliver has a world-wide fame. Prior to his time, the mine of Masonic archaeology had scarcely been worked; the publications in circulation scarcely exceeded half-a-dozen, and even these were by no means common in the country Lodges. The amount of research brought to bear on the subject undoubtedly created a spirit of enquiry, and led many to join the ranks of the craft. At the present-day, opinions vary considerably as to the value of many of Dr. Oliver's literary contributions. This is not to be wondered at, considering the vast range of Speculative Masonry, but it is yet a fact that no author's works are more frequently enquired for in a Masonic Library than his.

WILLIAM DIXON, P.M.

ADDITIONAL INFORMATION

He was the eldest son of Samuel Oliver, rector of Lambley, Nottinghamshire, by Elizabeth, daughter of George Whitehead, of Blyth Spital in the same county. He was born at Papplewick, Nottinghamshire, on 5 November 1782, and, after receiving a liberal education at Nottingham, he became in 1803 second master of Caistor grammar school. Six years afterwards, he was appointed to the headmastership of Grimsby grammar school.

Oliver was ordained deacon in 1813, and priest in 1814; and in July 1815 Bishop George Pretyman Tomline collated him to the living of Clee, when his name was placed on the boards of Trinity College, Cambridge, by Dr. Bayley, sub dean of Lincoln and examining chaplain to the bishop, as a ten-year man. In 1831, Bishop John Kaye gave him the rectory of Scopwick, Lincolnshire, which he held till his death. A Lambeth degree of D.D. was conferred on him on 25 July 1835.

From 1834 to 1846 Oliver was perpetual curate of St Peter's Collegiate Church, Wolverhampton. He was also a domestic chaplain to Lord Kensington. He had been elected deputy provincial grand master of masons for Lincolnshire in 1832, and in 1840 he was appointed an honorary member of the grand lodge of Massachusetts, with the rank of deputy grand master.

In 1846 Lord Lyndhurst, the Lord Chancellor, conferred on Oliver the rectory of South Hyckham, Lincolnshire, in return for vacating the curacy of Wolverhampton. In 1854 his voice began to fail, and, confiding the charge of his parishes to curates, he passed the remainder of his life in seclusion at Lincoln. There he died on 3 March 1867. He was buried on the 7th, with masonic rites, in the cemetery attached to the church of St. Swithin.

Oliver married in 1805 Mary Ann, youngest daughter of Thomas Beverley, by whom he left five children.

Masonic Writings
George Oliver

Select Writings of George Oliver from his various publications in his life time.

THE NUMBER THREE

The Science of Freemasonry embraces every branch of moral duty, whether it be applied to God, our neighbor, or ourselves. "A Mason is obliged, by his tenure, to obey the moral law; and if he rightly understands the art, he will never be a stupid atheist, nor an irreligious libertine." This peculiarity in the system is expressly inculcated on every member of the Order, at his first admission into a Lodge; so anxiously has Freemasonry provided against any mistake, as to its peculiar tenets. No Brother can be ignorant of the great points of Masonic duty, although he may be unacquainted with the minuter details. The traditions and peculiar doctrines which are included in the more abstruse portions of the Lectures, may have remained unexplored; but of its moral and religious tendency, he cannot be uninformed. The details of Wisdom are inscribed on its Tracing-board, in broad and indelible characters; and its general principles are so plain, that he who runs may read.

There is one distinguishing feature of the present age, which displays an increasing regard for the interests of morality. And the most auspicious anticipations of the ultimate prevalence of right principles may be entertained from this source alone. Even, in the absence of all the public institutions for the dissemination of useful knowledge, with which the present age abounds, this alone would proclaim the rapid progress of civilization, which can only be sound and useful, when found in connection with the practice of virtue. I allude to the prevalence of an anxiety for the increase of religious edifices for the worship of the Creator; and of Masonic halls for the inculcation of morals. Each of these sacred edifices hears a reference to the Temple of Solomon.

Thus, it was said of the Holy City of Jerusalem — "Very excellent things are spoken of thee, thou City of God." And well might excellent things be spoken of it; for it was not only placed in the center of a fertile country, and abounded in magnificent buildings; it was not only the seat of government, and the residence of the kings and princes of Judah; — it was not only the joy of the whole earth, in a civil and political point of view; but it was the abode of Jehovah; it contained his glorious Temple, where he was essentially present; where his altars burned with the purest sacrifices, and the priesthood dispensed his sacred word; where the High Priest was his chosen Oracle, through whom Divine responses were delivered; where the symbols of his glory were displayed, and where the Prince of Peace at length appeared in human form to work out the redemption of mankind.

In this holy City and Temple, we have a transcript of a Mason's Lodge. Like the City of God, our Lodge is founded on the mercies of Jehovah—consecrated in his name—dedicated to his honor—and from the foundation to the cope-stone, it proclaims "Glory to God in the highest, peace on earth, good-will towards men." The assemblies which are held within its walls, open their proceedings by invoking the name of the Most High; and after a course of mutual instruction in the morality which is most pleasing to Him, solemnly close their labors with prayer and thanksgiving.

The arrangement of the Lodge-room displays symbols of his power, and mercy, and goodness, in every quarter. In the east, west, and south, we discover tokens of his Omnipotence, in living emblems which refer to the wisdom, strength, and beauty displayed in the works of Creation. The way to another and a better world is designated by a symbol which rests on the Holy Bible, the foundation of our faith; and veils its superior glories in the cloudy canopy; while the All-Seeing Eye looks down upon us with complacency, as we are engaged in labors which purify the heart, and prepare it for a more exalted employment in the Grand Lodge above.

But there are many other peculiarities which identify a Freemason's Lodge with its acknowledged prototype, the city and temple of Jerusalem. The city was built on the high hills of Sion and Moriah, and near the deep valley of Jehosaphat; our Lodge is symbolically constructed on the highest of hills, or in the lowest of valleys. The temple was built due east and west—so is a Mason's Lodge.

The temple was an oblong square, and its ground was holy; such are the form and ground of the Lodge. The cherubim of the mercy-seat were surmounted by a cloud of glory; and, our Lodge, in like manner, is covered with a cloudy canopy. But not to dwell upon these coincidences, which, I confess, might have been accidental; I will refer as an unanswerable argument to prove the analogy between our Lodge room and the Temple of Solomon, to the triangular references which are common to both. The construction of the temple service embraced a multiplication of ternary allusions, which could only originate in divine revelations which had been communicated to man in the infancy of the world.

On Mount Moriah, where the three great offerings were consummated, three temples were successively constructed, each being furnished by the union of as many principles or powers. The first by Solomon and the two Hiram's, who represented the three Sephiroth—Wisdom, Strength, and Beauty. The second was erected under the superintendence of Zerubabel, Jeshua, and Haggai, who filled the three great offices of Jewish polity—Bang, Priest, and Prophet. The third by Herod, Hillel, and Shammai; who officiated as the three principal officers of the Lodge. The length of Solomon's Temple was three times its breadth; and the height and breadth of the second temple were each three-score cubits. It contained three courts; and the body of the temple consisted of three parts—the portico, the sanctuary, and the holy of holies. There were three curtains, each of three colors; three orders of priests; and three keepers of the door. The golden candlestick had three branches on each side; and there were three stones in each row of the high priest's breast-plate. The oxen which supported the molten sea, were arranged in threes, each triad looking towards one of the cardinal points, and the vessel was made of sufficient capacity to contain three thousand baths. To this holy place, the Jews were commanded to assemble three times a year, at the three grand festivals.

In the system of Freemasonry, the same process has been observed; and with the same symbolical reference. It displays clearly the analogy between a Mason's Lodge and the temple of Jehovah, in the city of God.

If we take a deliberate view of the Lodge, and consider, with a careful and scientific eye, its fundamental construction, we shall find that almost all its principal details are ternary. There are three degrees, three qualifications of a candidate, three traditional points, and three perfect points of entrance. The signs are commonly threefold: the steps—the principal officers—the moral duties—the theological virtues—the divine qualities inculcated in the principal points—all partake of the same character. The pillars that support the lodge, equally with the chief officers, are triangular. We have three greater and three lesser lights; three working tools for our Entered Apprentices; three qualifications for the servitude of an Apprentice, symbolized by chalk, charcoal, and clay; a ladder with as many principal steps; three ornaments; three articles of furniture; three moveable and three immoveable jewels, delta or trowel, which, when shaded, was the symbol of darkness, in the Hermesian hieroglyphics, and when open, of light; three colors, and three degrees. The reports are three-fold, as are also the principal orders of architecture. There are three grand offerings commemorated in the system of Freemasonry; the Entered Apprentices' duties are threefold; three places where the materials for the temple were prepared; and three sources where a knowledge of Operative Masonry is derived; three grand-masters; three officiating fellow-crafts; three decorations to the pillars at the porch of the temple, emblematical of peace, unity, and plenty; three ornaments of a Master's Lodge;

three different ways of opening a Lodge; three ways of preparing a brother; three obligations; three signs; three words; three tokens; and three ways to advance. We have also three Primitive Lodges; three temples; three principals; as many sojourners; three working tools; a triple triangle, and a delta sign, three greater and three lesser lights belonging to the Royal Arch. Indeed, the entire degree is founded on this significant emblem of the Deity. Then the three ineffable triads; the sign Golgotha; the equilateral triangles; and the triangular sconces of the encampment; with the three points; three columns; And three times three symbols of the Sacred Name in the Rose Croix, were also of the same character. In a word, wherever we cast our eyes, we discover the same reference to the triangle, that universal emblem of an Omnipotent Deity, characterized by infinite Wisdom, Strength, and Beauty and standing revealed to the Free and Accepted Mason in all his majesty and might.

In every age, and among all people, whether their religion were true or false, this remarkable attachment to the number Three hate been found to prevail. The early patriarchs included a triad of offices m their own person; for each was the king, priest, and prophet of his family and tribe; an arrangement which has been perpetuated in the system of Freemasonry, and embodied in one of its highest and most sublime degrees. Three men communed with Abraham under the oak at Mamre. In the Conciliator, a Jewish commentary on the books of the Old Testament, by the Rabbi Manasseh ben Israel, for which I am indebted to Brother Turner, of Grantham, the number three is made good use of on several occasions. The Rabbi says: "The three patriarchs are likened to the heavenly bodies—Abraham to the Sun as rising in the east—Isaac to the Moon, as receiving his light from him—and Jacob to the Zodiac, from his sons constituting so many stars. Therefore, in Bamidmar-Raba, these appellations are given to them. Descending from the heavens to the firmament, the seven planets come after the orbs. These correspond to the seven pre-eminent men until Jacob, i.e., Adam, Seth, Noah, Shem, Abraham, Isaac, and Jacob; or, according to others, commencing with Jacob, it will be, Levi, Kohath, Amram,

Moses, Aaron, David, and Solomon; or, Abraham, Isaac, Jacob, Moses, Aaron, David, and Solomon. In either way, this number is mystical; for as the sun has three planets above his orb, Mars, Jupiter, and Saturn; and three below it, the Moon, Venus, and Mercury; so, Moses is compared to the sun from being in the center of these last enumeration of patriarchs. Therefore, our sages say, the face of Moses shone like the sun."

Mount Sinai, or Horeb, which was selected by the Almighty as the site of a divine manifestation, had three tops of a marvelous height, says Sandeys, on one of which God appeared to Moses in the burning bush; on another he delivered the Law; and the lowest is now called Mount Catherine, from a monastery at its foot, dedicated to that saint. Under the Mosaic dispensation, a man had three duties to perform towards his wife. The principal annual festivals of the Jews were three—the Passover—to preserve the memory of their redemption from the bondage of Egypt; the Pentecost, in commemoration of the delivery of the Law from Sinai; and the feast of Tabernacles, in remembrance of their miraculous preservation in the wilderness. The camp, or army of Israel, is said to have been three-fold. The tabernacle with its precinct was called "the camp of the Divine Majesty;" the next, "the camp of Levi, or little host of the Lora;" and the largest, "the camp of Israel, or the great host." The tabernacle had three divisions, and three symbolical references—historical, mystical, and moral. The golden candlestick had twice three branches, each containing three bowls, knops, and flowers. In the sanctuary were three sacred utensils, the candlestick, the table of shew-bread, and the altar of incense; and three hallowed articles were deposited by the Ark of the Covenant in the Holy of Holies, viz. the tables of the law, the rod of Aaron, and the pot of manna. There were three orders of priests and Levites, and the high priest was distinguished by a triple crown.

Moses appointed, by divine authority, three cities of refuge; forbad the people to use the fruit of their newly planted trees till after they were three years old; and made three witnesses necessary to establish a fact by which the life or property of any individual was brought into question. The form of benediction was tripartite; and was considered of sufficient importance to warrant its subsequent introduction into Christian baptism. In the remarkable history of Balaam, the ass spake after having been struck three times; and the prophet conferred on Israel three separate blessings. Samson thrice deceived Dalilah. Hannah, the mother of Samuel, offered a sacrifice of three bullocks, when she dedicated her son to the service of the tabernacle. Samuel gave a sign to Saul consisting of a combination of triads. David bowed thrice before Jonathan. He had three mighty men of valor; and placed the Ark of the Covenant in the house of Obed Edom for three months. When he had numbered the people, he was offered three alternatives, viz., three years of famine, three months at the mercy of his foes, or three days of pestilence. Solomon offered sacrifices three times a year. At the building of the temple, this number was peculiarly exemplified. There were three grand masters; three places where the materials were prepared; and the edifice at three divisions. Amongst the workmen were—Harodim, 300; Menatzchim, 3300; Adoniram, 30,000; master masons, 3600, &c. And the dimensions of the temple were in exact proportion with the three concords in music. The height was 30 cubits, and the length three times greater than the breadth. The harmony and symmetry of these three dimensions were as grateful to the eye, as harmony in music was ravishing to the ear.

Once more, Elijah raised the widow's son by stretching himself upon the child three times. Samaria sustained a siege of three years. Some of the kings of Israel and Judah reigned three years; some three months; and others only three days. Rehoboam served God three years before he apostatized. The Jews fasted three days and three nights by command of Esther, before their triumph over Haman. Their sacred writings had three grand divisions: the Law, the Prophets, and the Psalms. According to our Masonic system, there were three temples, those of Solomon, Zerubbabel, and Herod. The Jews reckon only two, arid believe that the third, as described by

Ezekiel the prophet, is yet to come. The Rabbi Manasseh ben Israel says, "the third temple we hope and look for." And after enumerating three times seven circumstances as then existing, which were not in the temple of Zerubbabel, he goes on to say, "much more might be urged in proof of this third temple, but I shall only note the remarkable allegory of the three wells dug by Isaac's servants, to which they gave different names. To the first, Contention, from the quarrel they had respecting it; to the second, Hatred, for the same reason; and to the third, Extension, because the Lord extended to them the hope of peopling the land; an appropriate symbol of the three temples; walls of living waters of the law, and the abundance of divine influence; where against the first Nebuchadnezzar made war; Titus against the second; but in the third, all will be prosperous; as Isaiah says, Extend the place of thy tent more than ever, for the Lord will ever inhabit it And the name of the city from that day shall be—the Lord is there."

And even in things apparently indifferent, the same machinery was carefully maintained. Adam, Noah, and Saul, had each three sons. There were three patriarchs, particularly distinguished by the divine favor before the birth of the twelve tribes of Israel, Job had three friends. The just men, quoted by Ezekiel, were three in number; three holy men were cast by Nebuchadnezzar into the furnace at Babylon; Jonah was three days and three nights in the whale's belly; and at the transfiguration of Christ, the same number of holy men appeared in conversation with him. On one occasion, our Savior refers to the Tetragrammaton by a triple allusion. And the Jewish symbols of the same name were all tripartite. The Redeemer remained three days in the tomb; and Paul was blind for the same period after the revelation of his mission. The same apostle mentions three heavens and three states of the soul. And to close these coincidences, the heavenly Jerusalem of the Apocalypse has three gates in each of its quarters. So universal was the use and application of the number three in the three dispensations of truth—the Patriarchal, the Jewish, and the Christian.

THE NUMBER THREE

The Rabbins say there are three lights in God; the ancient, pure, and purified lights; and that the world was created by a threefold union of Wisdom, Goodness, and Power. The author of the Book of Zohar applies the word holy, which is there repeated in the vision of Isaiah, to the three persons in the Deity, whom he elsewhere calls three suns, or lights; three sovereigns, without beginning and without end. It is asserted in the Talmud that God has three keys, viz., of the rain, the womb, and the grave. They believe in three states of the soul, three worlds, and three temples of God. The mystical sense of Scripture was considered to be of three kinds, corresponding with the three theological virtues—Faith, which was termed allegorical; Hope, tropological; and Charity, anagogical. For instance, of the word Jerusalem, which was the chief city in Judea: allegorically, it meant the church-militant; tropologically, a true believer's rejoicing in hope; and anagogically, the church triumphant in heaven. Again, the word light in the first chapter of Genesis, evidently means material light; but allegorically it referred to the Messiah, who is hence called by Zechariah and St. Luke, Oriens; in a tropological sense, it signifies the divine grace; and anagogically, the glorious and eternal Light of heaven. Even the roots of Hebrew words are, with few exceptions, of three letters, forming the third person singular masculine, in allusion to the Deity, whose eternal existence is all we know of him, i.e. He is, He was, He will be; comprised in the three letters היה.

In every spurious system of religion, the same veneration for this remarkable number will be found to prevail. It was not only considered possessing many mystical properties, but was esteemed divine. The Hermetical secrets were modeled on the number three, or the equilateral triangle, as an emblem of their reputed founder, who concealed the mysteries of religion under hieroglyphics and allegories, and exposed nothing to the eyes of the vulgar, but the beauties of his morality. These mysteries were communicated only to those who had been solemnly initiated into his spurious Freemasonry. The potent instrument by which the hierophants executed their cabalistical performances, was a magical rod set with precious stones, and having three heads of silver. If any initiated person revealed the secrets of the order, he was sure to die within three days. Such was the belief; and therefore, it is probable they never were divulged till after the sacerdotal influence had ceased. It sufficiently proves, however, the great care with which their secrets were concealed. They said, these things are coming down from our father Adam, Seth, and Hermes or Enoch the triple. "The candidate, at his initiation, appears to have been enclosed for a considerable time in a coffin, or chest, while the hierophant performed certain preliminary ceremonies. He then smote the lid of the coffin three times with his divining rod; and after the aspirant had entered into the usual engagements, he was raised from a figurative state of death to life, and received amongst the wise and learned sons of science."

Pythagoras learned the elements of his numerical system, as he himself informs us, when he was initiated at Libeth, in Thrace, by Agliophemus. By the use of numbers, he framed his canon of divination. His pupil Abaris practiced it after the custom of the barbarians, by victims, principally of cocks, whose entrails he conceived most proper for the purpose; but Pythagoras, unwilling to take him off from the study of truth, directed him, by a safer method, without blood or slaughter, divination by numbers, considering that to be more sacred, and agreeable to the nature of the gods.

He taught his disciples that the triad is the first number actually odd, and the first perfect number, the middle and proportion; for which reason oracles were delivered from a tripod, and libations were three-fold. He said that all things are governed by harmony; which is a system consisting of three concords: the diatessaron, the diapente, and the diapason. And these consonances are constituent parts of the Tetractys, or sacred name of God. He reduced all beings to real ideas; and those to ideas of ideas. Hence his notion of three worlds—the inferior, the superior, and the supreme; and Aristotle says he held that all things whatever are terminated by three. Number was considered to be of two kinds, intellectual and sciential.

The former was termed, "the eternal substance of number; the principle most providential of all heaven and earth, and the nature that is betwixt them. It is the principle, fountain, and root of all things. It existed before all other things in the divine mind; and out of it all things were digested into order, and remain numbered by an indissoluble series."

The sciential was subdivided into two sorts; the former limited, the latter infinite. In this respect, the Pythagoreans differed from the Platonists, who deemed all numbers to be infinite. Odd numbers were esteemed more propitious than even ones; and hence were the conservators of greater virtues. They were sacred to the celestial deities, and represented the male sex, while even numbers were female, and appropriated to the subterranean gods. Hence, the monad was esteemed the father of number, and the duad the mother; from whose union proceeded, not only the triad but the sacred quaternary, which was the origin of the seven liberal sciences, and the maker and cause of all things. From the divine nature of number, Pythagoras considered it to be eternal in its substance; the most provident principle in the universe; and the root of human and divine beings; the monad being the cause, and the duad the effect. Thus, the monad and duad were the phallus and kties of the Greeks, the lingam and yoni of the Hindoos, the woden and friga of the Goths, the yang and yin of the Chinese, and indeed of the creative and destructive powers of every country under heaven.

In his system of practical philosophy, the number three appears to have been profusely used. The geometricians, not being able to express incorporeal forms by words, had recourse to the description of figures, saying this △ is a triangle; not only this which falls under the sight, but that which hath the same figure, because it represents the knowledge of a triangle to the mind. In moral geometry, a triangle is an emblem of friendship; the equilateral triangle symbolizing perfect friendship. The base being taken as a duty, the perpendicular will be the security of performance, and the hypotenuse the advantage arising from it; whence, if the duty of sincerity flow equally, the advantage will also flow equally. The Pythagoreans adopted the same course in the elements of science; for as they could not express in words incorporeal forms 5 and first principles, they had recourse to demonstration by numbers. Thus, they constructed the numerical triad; which they called Heaven, Earth, Middle Nature. Virtue was defined by a triad, viz., Pedeutic, Politic, Physic; and out of the former, they constructed a double triad, of commendable qualities: Institution, Silence, Abstinence, and Fortitude, Temperance, Sagacity. Institution was then explained by the new triad of Wisdom, Magnanimity, Fortitude. The system of silence was quinquennial; and the neophyte was enjoined to repeat this verse mentally, morning and evening:

> "Suffer not sleep at night to close thine eyes.
> Till thrice thy acts that day thou hast o'errun,
> How slipt? What deeds, what duty left undone?"

Abstinence was recommended, so far as might be safely practiced, from wine, meat, sleep. In his theory of the virtue of Temperance, Pythagoras used a complication of triads. Thus, he said, if we listen to the language of the flesh, we shall hear it cry out, no hunger, no thirst, no cold; but it is better to amputate, by all practical means, from the body, soul, belly,—all sickness, ignorance, luxury; and from the city, family, all things, sedition, discord, excess. Of Sagacity, he gave this triad: Wisdom is the strength, wall, armor of man. The Hexad, he said, proceeded from a combination of the first even and the first odd number; for as all mankind proceeded from a male and female, so this number is generated of 3, a male, and 2, a female; for 3 x 2 = 6. And hence the Hexad was denominated Triaditis, because it assumes the three motions of intervals. The Hexad indicates time, consisting of three parts—past, present, and to come, because it is formed of equal triads. In like manner, the Ennead **(A group or set of nine)** is the square of the first odd number 3; and hence is called Horizon, because the number hath nothing beyond it; Prometheus, because it is a perfect ternary, because it is the first odd triangle.

The great secret communicated by Pythagoras to his disciples was the method of finding out the nature of the Deity by the resolution of the triad into the monad, which formed the sacred Tetractys, or God: equivalent with the Jewish Tetragrammaton, or Self-Existent,* which he termed the number of numbers; and it constituted the obligation by which his aspirants were enjoined to secrecy. The process by which the result was developed as follows:

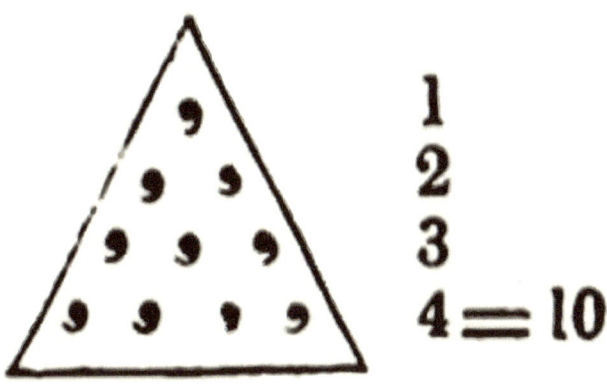

*This doctrine is illustrated in the construction of the Decalogue, which consists of Ten Commandments, the first four of which relate exclusively to the Divine Giver. And in Masonry, it is exemplified in the ten mathematical characters which constituted the mark of Hiram Abiff.

These were the words —

> "By that pure, holy four letter nabik on high.
> Nature's eternal fountain and supply.
> The parent of all souls that living be.
> By him, with faithful oath, I swear to thee."

Thus, the number ten was produced, which was esteemed the greatest number, and comprehended all arithmetical and harmonical proportions. It was called World, because, as the decad comprehends all numbers, so the world comprehends all forms; Heaven, because it is perfect; because it includes all the nature of even and odd, good and evil. The emblematical triangle represented the Deity residing in heaven, which, being the most perfect place, is here designated by the most perfect number.

Pythagoras thus demonstrated how the number ten proceeded from the number three. The triad is the first perfect number, and produces the three other perfect numbers. Thus, 3 + 1 gives the tetrad, or tetractys; 3 + 4 produces the heptad, which was denominated worthy of veneration; 3 + 7 gives the decad, or sacred number Ten. This is the end of all numbers, and, as the Rabbi Judah a Levi, very justly observes in various places, contains a wonderful secret.

CHAPTER II

If the doctrines of Pythagoras were to be traced through all the combinations of which they are susceptible, Number would be found to constitute the alpha and omega of his system, and the Number Three would be the tripod whence all his oracles proceed. And the same excellence which this philosopher ascribed to numbers, the Free and Accepted Mason attributes to geometrical symbols. Pythagoras concludes that "in the nature of things exists something, which hath beginning, middle, and end. To such a form and nature, he attributes the number three, saying that whatsoever hath a middle is tri-form, so he called every perfect thing. And whatever is perfect useth this principle, and is adorned according to it. This was expressed by the Triad; and when he endeavored to bring his disciples to the knowledge thereof, it was accomplished by the form of this Triad."

The number three was a symbol of marriage, friendship, peace, and concord; because it collects and unites, not similars, but contraries. It was also an emblem of wisdom and prudence; because men order the present, foresee the future, and learn experience from the past. Hence, the number three was said to extend its influence to all nature, and to comprehend all terrestrial things, by embracing the birth-life-death of men and animals, the commencement-middle-end of all earthly matters; and the past-present-future of universal space. It constitutes "the Seal of the First Cause, who is truth itself, for his being alone is true, and not dependent on another cause. For this reason, Truth is a moral virtue that ought to be esteemed, since, as Abarbanel observes on Zech iii. 8, 9, it includes every active precept, and every theological virtue."

The Greeks had a high veneration for odd numbers, because it was thought that *numero deus impare gaudet*; (**God loves odd numbers**) and for the number three in particular. They divided their deities into three classes—the celestial, the terrestrial, and the infernal. Triptolemus left behind him three primary laws—honor to parents, against bloody offerings, against cruelty to animals. Democritus wrote a book to prove that all human things sprang from the number three, and called it Trilogenia. The same people used this number as a charm for the dead. Thus Zachary Bogan, in the Archceologiae Atticae says, "next to the happiness of being buried, was that of being buried in their own country. Insomuch, that if a man died so far from home, that they could not come to the body, they were wont, with solemn and frequent invocations, naming him thrice at every time, to give a shout for the soul: which they thought was still quick enough to come to them. Pindar says that Phrixus, when he was dying at Colchis, desired Pelias to see this office performed for him. And so, Ulysses, after he had lost three score and twelve of his company among the Cicones, made it his business, as Homer tells us, to give a whoop for everyone, three times. Theocritus says the same thing of Hylas; and one in the Ranis of Aristophanes says concerning the dead, they are gone so far that you cannot reach them at thrice calling."

The ancient mystics carried their veneration for this number so far as to reject the earth as an element for the purpose of introducing it; thereby making three elements only: viz., fire, air, water; which were termed the mothers of nature. Thus, it was asserted that heaven was created from fire and earth from water; the air being the medium of correspondence between them. Again, they taught the doctrine of three primitive qualities-heat, cold, moisture; and that extreme heat proceeding from fire, and extreme cold from water, it was only by the interposition of air that a proper temperature can be produced in the earth, to render it fit for the habitation of man. And in the human frame, the same principles were enunciated. The head was fire, as being the region of thought; the body, water, because it is material and corruptible; and the mind, air, or spirit.

They held that the universe contains three worlds, which are termed Knowledge, Wisdom, Perfection: corresponding with the earth, the firmament or sidereal world, and heaven, or the dwelling place of the Deity. In another sense, these worlds are called angelic, celestial, corruptible, and deemed correlative with the three principal functions of the human body, which are seated respectively in the brain, heart, liver. In the Hebrew language, the Sun had three different names, referring to its orb, light, flame. The universe was divided into three zones—the earth, air, rest. The first was the earth, or zone of trial; the second was the zone of the air, perpetually agitated by winds and storms, and was considered as the zone of temporal punishment; and the third was the zone of rest and tranquility, which was above the other two. Thus was the number three modified in the mystical cabala of antiquity.

The seat of the celestial deities, called Olympus, wholly lucid, was erected on the number three, and its summit was unity; although the mountain with three peaks was usually esteemed most holy. And hence the solar sacrifices were placed on three contiguous piles of wood. The Druids of Britain and Gaul, like all other people, held this number sacred, and many of their peculiar customs, founded on this belief, still remain. Borlase says, "in the isle of Skie, after drinking the water of a famous well there, they make three Sun-turns round the well, as if some deity resided in it, to whom they were to pay proper respect before they left it. Weak and simple as these turns may seem, they have been used by the most ancient, and the most polite nations, and in the same number as now practiced by these uncultivated highlanders. They turn three times round their karns; **(A pile of rocks (Cairn)** round the persons they intend to bless three times; three turns they make round St. Barr's church, and three turns round the well; so that the number three was a necessary part of the ceremony." The British bards mention three fountains which ought to be venerated—that of the sea or salt water, rain, and fresh springs flowing from the rock.

Thus, we find the number three exemplified in physics throughout the whole ancient world; and particularly in the Patriarchal and Jewish systems of religion, which were honored by the Almighty with especial manifestations of his will and pleasure. The question then arises: How are we to account for the universal use and application of this remarkable number? Having been venerated in the earliest ages of the world, it must have proceeded from the Creator himself. And accordingly, the equilateral triangle has always been considered by every person, nation, and language, as an indication of the Great Architect of the Universe. It is, indeed, a symbol of perfection; and is hence made by the continental Masons to represent our mortal career, as consisting of birth, life, and death. And there appears much propriety in the arrangement, so far as it alludes to Freemasonry, which includes everything that is valuable to man in his progress from this world to the next.

Now the universal predilection for the number three being thus applied to the Deity by the earliest inhabitants of the world, could not fail to bear a reference to the doctrine of a plurality of persons in the Godhead; known probably at the Creation, and transmitted to posterity by oral tradition, confirmed and strengthened by the ordinances of the Most High, which were usually, in their form and spirit, of a ternary nature. This doctrine was too profound for the apprehension of those persons whose ideas wandered amongst sensible objects, in their search for the essence of the Deity. And hence it will be seen, from an accurate examination of the principles which constituted the triads of all nations, that how imperceptible soever the shades of error might be, in its downward progress, by the innovations of successive hierophants and mystagogues, the original purport of the doctrine became perverted in the Spurious Freemasonry, until the true meaning was misunderstood, and applied to purposes altogether foreign to its primitive import.

Sir W. Jones thought it little short of blasphemy to refer the heathen triads to the Trinity of the Patriarchal, Jewish, and Christian churches; but I think, with due deference to such a high authority, that it is not more profane to believe that a tradition of the Trinity was incorporated into the Spurious Freemasonry of ancient times, than that the same institution was a depository of the Unity; and I agree with Bishops Horsley and Tomline, the indefatigable Cudworth, who terms the Triplasian Mithras "a trinity in the

Persian theology, or three hypostases in one and the same deity," Sonnerat, Acosta, Le Compte, Forster, Maurice, Hutchinson, and many other wise and learned men, in believing that the origin of all the various triads which existed in the Gentile world, may be consistently traced to the primitive belief in a trinity of hypostases which constitute the God-head; and the heathen triad is even denominated by the erudite Purchas, "an apish imitation of the trinity, brought in by the devil."

Mr. Faber contests the point. He observes—"if Brahma—Vishnu—Siva, relate to the trinity, it will not be easy to assign a reason why they should be represented as springing from a fourth or superior god." I am persuaded, however, that this is only a perverted representation of the primitive doctrine of a trinity in unity; or, as it was more philosophically expressed, according to the oracle in Damascius, the triad resolved into a monad; which the British Druids carried out dramatically in their initiations. The hierophant who personated the deity, represented the monad; and he was attended by three priests to represent the triad; and three hymns were sung in the holy sanctuary when the rites were completed.

Being known to Noah and his family, this doctrine would spread with every migration of their posterity: and as it certainly formed a part of that original system of Light which is now termed Freemasonry, so it was introduced into every perversion of that system, until the doctrine of a divine triad resolving itself into a monad—or as Lucian truly expresses it, although in jest, was universally disseminated in every nation, and admitted by every people in the world. Its invention was ascribed to Cronus, another name for Noah, or perhaps Ham, for the identity is uncertain. And in the oracles of the first Zoroaster, which are of an unknown antiquity, we find the principle enunciated. *"A Triad of Deity shines throughout the world, of which a monad is the head."* In successive ages, the true purport was misunderstood, but the principle remained, though its application ceased to be made to the true God and Father of all; and was generally transferred to the three sons of Noah, as a triplication of the mortal father of the human race.

Mr. Maurice traces the idea in the Gentile world to a perversion of Jewish hieroglyphics. He says, "the illuminated heads, the innumerable eyes, and the extended wings of the cherubic beings, which, in the Jewish hieroglyphics, ever accompanied that refulgent symbol, were doubtless intended to represent the guardian vigilance of the Supreme Providence, as well as the celerity of the motions of that celestial light and spirit which pervades and animates all nature. The innocent and expressive emblem, which devotion had originally formed, was caught up and debased in the pagan world. The fire, light, and spirit which, among the former, were only typical of the Supreme Being, and his attributes, were by them mistaken for the Supreme Being, and were accordingly venerated in the place of that Being. These three principles became inextricably involved in their theology, and inseparably incorporated in all their systems of philosophy. They called the elementary fire, Ptha, Vulcan, Agnee; the solar light, they denominated Osiris or Mithra, Surya, Apollo; and the pervading air, or spirit, Cneph, Marayen, Zeus, or Jupiter. Under those and other names, they paid their divine homage; and thus, having, by degrees, from some dark ill-understood notions of a real trinity in the Divine Nature, united to that mysterious doctrine their own romantic speculations in the vast field of physics, they produced a degraded trinity, the sole fabrication of their fancy; and instead of the God of Nature, nature itself, and the various elements of nature, became the objects of their blind and infatuated devotion."

The principal religious triads in the heathen world were as follows; — The Egyptian, of Trismegistus, or Osiris — Isis — Orus — and Eicton — Cneph — Phtba; the Orphic, of Phanes — Uranus — Cronus; or, according to some authorities, Thos — Boule — Zoe; the Magian, of the Triplasian Mithras, or Ormisda — Mithra — Ahriman; the Indian, of Brahma — Vishnu — Siva, and Balrama — Subhadra — Jaganath; the Cabiric, of Axieros — Axiokersa — Axiokersos; the Phoenician, of Ashtaroth — Milcom —

Chemosh; the Tyrian, of Belus Venus — Thammuz; the Grecian and Roman, of Jupiter — Neptune — Pluto; the Eleusinian, of Bacchus — Proserpine — Ceres; the Cyclopean, of Brontes — Steropes — Arges; the Thracian, of Uranus — Urania — Love; the Platonic, of Tagathon — Nous — Psyche; the Tartar, of Artugon — Schugoteugon — Tangara: the Celtic, of HuCeridwen — Creirwy; the Teutonic, of Fenris — Midgard — Hela; the Gothic, of Woden — Friga — Thor; the Scandinavian, of Odin — Vile — Ve; the Peruvian, of Tangatanga; the Mexican, of Vitzliputzli — Tlaloc — Tescalipuca.

Each triad was generally explained to consist of a creator, a preserver, and a destroyer; or, according to Maurice, a renovator; and this doctrine was embodied in another feature of the Spurious Freemasonry, viz., the belief in an endless succession of similar grand periods, called worlds; each of which was supposed to be in constant progress towards destruction; after which a new creation invariably takes place. And thus the operations of one or other member of the triad are always in active exercise, in the successive works of renovation, preservation, or destruction.

But if the triad, as an illustration of the number three, was thus the foundation of religion, it was also disseminated in detail through every branch of the system. In some nations, this triple form of the divinity was convertible under a change of circumstances. Thus, in universal nature, it was denominated by the Greeks, Phoebus — Phoebe — Pan; in the elements, Vulcan — Juno — Neptune; in the prolific power which produces fruits, &c., Bacchus — Ceres — Vertumnus; and in the infernal regions, Pluto — Proserpine — Minos. In subsequent ages, the Emperor Julian, who was not ignorant of the Christian's trinity, constituted a new triad, which he called Sol — Monimus — Azizus.

The notion of a triple intelligence so far pervaded the mythology of Greece and Rome, that it became of universal application; for the number three was supernal, and it was not considered possible for any system, either of philosophy or divinity, to be constructed without its assistance. Thus, *Jupiter* was distinguished by the three-forked lightning; Neptune, by the trident; Pluto, by Cerberus, the triple-headed dog; while the caduceus of Mercury assumed a triform character, either by the central circle, with upper and lower semicircles attached, or by the wand flanked with serpents' heads. Sometimes this appendage was represented merely as a winged pedestal surmounted by the two intersecting serpents, which still embodied a complete triad; for the serpents formed a circle and lunette, to represent the sun and moon, and the wings were the hovering spirit of the elements. Hence, Homer terms this symbolical instrument "the golden three-leaved rod." There was also a triad of Graces, called Aglia — Thalia — Euphrosyne; another of Fates, named Clotho — Lachesis — Atropos; of Sirens, called Parthenope — Ligea — Leucosia; and of Furies, who were denominated Alecto — Tisiphone — Megara. Even the obscene deities were invested with the same dignity. Thus, they had a triad of Priapus — Phallus — Fascinus; of Harpies, called Aello — Ocypete — Celeno; and of Gorgons, named Medusa — Stheno — Euryale. "In the 54th plate of Montfaucon's Supplement, in his account of Gaulic Antiquities, may be seen assemblages of deities in triple groups. In one of these groups, it is not a little remarkable that the center figure hath shoes on his feet, as if of superior dignity; the other two figures, as if subordinate, are barefooted.

In Gruter, too, may be seen deities in triple groups, worshipped by the ancient Germans which they call Mairae, and one is thus inscribed, in *honorem domus divince diis Mairabus*." **(In honor of the divine house, to the Goddesses Mairai)**

Again, the Orphic Cronus was compounded of a man, a lion, and a serpent; the Chimaera, of a serpent, a lion, and a goat; and while Hecate was represented with three human bodies conjoined, Orion was reputed to have had three fathers. Cicero mentions three Anactes, whom he calls Tritopateus—Eubuleus—Dionysus. The three steps by which Neptune is represented by Homer to have crossed the horizon, and the three steps of Vishnu, in his fifth avater, might have a similar reference; as also the teeth of Scylla, the Bacchic trieterica, the tripos of Apollo, the German trigla, the Celtic cromlech, or trilithic edifices of Britain and Gaul, and the triple division of the universe into heaven, earth, and hell; where the moon, in the former, was termed Diana; in the next, Luna; and in the latter, Hecate. Pausanias relates that the statue of Jupiter, which was removed from the palace of Priam, when Troy was sacked, had three eyes, in allusion, to his triple government of heaven, hell, and the waters. And Lycophron calls Hercules Triesper.

The mysterious veneration which the ancients entertained for the number three, was manifested in every part of their mystical theology. Thus, the statue of Diana, in common with those of Serapis, Geryon, Chimaera, the Sphynx, the Indian dog of Yama, Trisiras, the American deity Bochica, and the tricipital of all nations, was sometimes represented with three heads, viz., of a horse, a dog, and a man; or a bull, a dog, and a lion; and the following lines expressed her properties under this threefold character:

Ter ret, lustrat, agit,— Proserpina, Luna, Diana,
Ima, suprema, feros, — sceptro, fulgore, sagitta.
And again in the Æneid:
Tergeminamque Hecatem, tria virginis ora Diane.

Each head was surmounted by the *Tau Cross*, and the body terminated in the folds of a double serpent. With a similar allusion Milton said, The Moon—her countenance tri-form, Hence tills and empties, to enlighten the earth.

There was also a colossal statue of Hercules called Trihesperus (sprung from the triad of night), which is mentioned in a fragment of Nicetas of Choniate. The Athenians had an altar sacred to Shame—Fame— Impetuosity, and the sacrifices were all tri-form. The Megarenses placed in the temple of Venus an image of Love— Imeros—Pothos; and at Corinth was a triple statue of Jupiter, the first being deemed nameless, the second was called Terrestrial, and the third Most High. In the temple of Diana at the same place was a monument of Pittheus, on which were three thrones; and near the theater was a temple with three altars, dedicated to Bacchus, Themis, and the Sun. These extracts are from Pausanias, who mentions other temples in which the triad was worshipped. In one, Bacchus—Ceres—Proserpine; in another, Apollo — Minerva—Proserpine; and in a third, Zephyrus—Minerva—Neptune, were united objects of adoration. In the temple of Fortune at Thebes, in Boeotia, was a triad of ancient statues of Venus, in her characters of Celestial—Popular—Apostrophia; and Herodotus refers to another in a floating island near Buto, consecrated to Apollo, which had a triad of altars. Mandesloe mentions a square pillar in a temple at Mardasch, with the figure of a monarch worshipping a triad, consisting of Sun— Fite—Serpent. The Romans carried the same principle into all their social institutions, whether civil, military, or religious: the number three constituting a sort of universal principle to which perfection was attached. Hence their Tribunes and Triumvirs; their Castra Tertiata and Triarii; their Trifax and Triobolum; their Triens and their Triga; their Trivium and Triremis, and other matters which originated in a superstitious regard for the ternary form.

In the mysteries of India, the doctrine of the trinity was clearly expressed, f but its meaning was rather equivocal; and it is a question whether the first person in the triad was esteemed to be the true God, or only an emanation from the doctrine of an endless succession of worlds; and consequently a personification of Adam or Noah, who were equally worshipped under the common name of Brahma, or the creative power, because the parent of mankind; for Brahma was only a created being. In truth, Brahma appears to have been Adam or Noah; and the triad Brahma—Vishnu—Siva, expressed by the tri-literal monosyllable **AUM**, was either Abel, Seth, Cain, or Shem, Japheth, Ham; for there exist considerable doubts, after all, whether this being, to whom the rites of Hindu adoration were so devoutly paid, was not a mere deified mortal.

Still, there is a difficulty in reconciling this conjecture with the uniform language of their sacred books, which ascribe infinite perfection to each member of the triad. Thus, in the concluding book of the Ramayuna, Vishnu is described as "the being of beings— one substance in three forms; without mode, without quality, without passion; immense, incomprehensible, infinite, indivisible, immutable, incorporeal, irresistible. His operations no mind can conceive, and his will moves all the inhabitants of the universe, as puppets are moved by strings." In remembrance of this triad, they wore a sacred Zennar, or cord of three threads, next to their bodies; whence the number three has been holden by them in the most sacred veneration through every period of their existence as a nation.

CHAPTER III

In these dissertations on the mystical Number Three, I have condensed my materials into the smallest compass. The subject is inexhaustible: volumes would not contain it. But I have designedly comprised my observations within the characteristic number of THREE papers. I proceed therefore with a detail of the extraordinary coincidences of this Number in China, where the same regard for its occult properties appears to have prevailed. Indeed, the Chinese entertained a most superstitious veneration for odd numbers generally, as containing divine properties. Thus, while the sum of the even numbers 2 + 4 + 6 + 8 + 10 = 30 designated the number of Earth, the sum of the odd numbers 1 + 3 + 5 + 7 + 9 = 25 was dignified with the appellation of the number of *Heaven*. And they say *Tao* or *Reason*, produced *one*; one produced *two*; two produced *three*; and three produced all things. They had a talisman in the form of an equilateral triangle, which was reputed to afford protection in all cases of personal danger and adversity. The mystical symbol Y was also much esteemed, from its allusion to the triune Deity; the three distinct lines of which it is composed forming one, and the one is three. And the sacred ceremony of the Kow-tow was performed by three times three prostrations.

An ancient institution has been recently discovered in China which is called Tieu-ti-huih, the Triad Society, or Peach Garden Association. It has been called, by the Chinese, according to Newbold and Wilson, "the three united, from being composed of the members of a sacred triad, viz., Heaven—Earth—Man, to whom equal adoration is offered, being all considered of equal dignity and rank; but to man only after death, under the name of ancestors. Heaven and earth are worshipped as the father and mother of mankind. They are styled the three dominant powers and supposed to exist in perfect harmony. There appears to be some mystical importance attached to the number *Three* by the Chinese. Three is the number of the officials, or elder brethren; of the drops of blood which are shed during the inaugural rites; of their days of meeting during the month, and of the prescribed prostrations before the idol, *viz.*, *pae*, *kwei*, and *koto*, bowing, kneeling, and placing the forehead in the dust; the last, in some ceremonies, is thrice repeated. The grand day is the ninth of the moon, equal to three times three. The secret manual signs are made with three fingers. The characters on some of the mystical seals are grouped into triads. One of them is in the form of a triangle. The symbol on another appears to have been selected for its triune character, resembling the trisula of the Hindus; and three is generally the number of the personages forming the group in the picture worshipped by almost every Chinese." To the above very clear account of the use of the number Three in China, we may add that the Sacred Books delivered to *Chang Kiok* by a messenger from Heaven were three; and a passage in the oath of the Society commences, "Let us swear to be like the ancient and sacred Society of the three surnames. Heaven is father; earth is mother; ancestors are stems; children and grand-children are leaves. Trees have a root; waters have a fountain. The stem, flowers and fruit all spring from the root."

The Egyptians, with whom the triad appears to have been more distinctly understood, used the equilateral triangle as a symbol of their numen, the threefold deity; and placed another expressive emblem over the portals of their temples, *viz.*, Globe—Serpent—Wings; while the Druids of Britain constructed entire temples of this form. The most ancient of the Cabiri or Dioscori, had a temple at Memphis; and are said by Cicero to have been in number three; and their names Tretopatraeus, Eubuleus, and Dionysius. All that can be with truth averred concerning them is, that they were esteemed as the Three mighty guardian genii of the Universe, or rather the various parts of that universe physically considered, and that they were worshipped in Samothracia with rites which were among the most mysterious and profound in all antiquity. One curious circumstance, however, concerning them it is in my power to relate; for as Hecate, from her threefold nature or office, was honored in Greece with an anniversary festival, celebrated in a place where three ways met, so were the Anakes, or gods Cabiri, honored with another, called from them, Anakea. The sacrifices offered at this solemnity, says Potter, in his account of the Grecian festivals, were called Zenismot, because those deities were strangers, and they consisted of three offerings.

The hieroglyphical device, says a modern writer, styled *Vesica Piscis* **(A pointed oval figure used as an architectural feature)** appertained to the Platonic system. Plato and Proclus refer repeatedly to this figure, which they had seen and heard interpreted in Egypt. It often appears on the temples, and especially on the throne of Osiris. It referred to the doctrine of the Egyptian priests on the subject of their trinity, and represented geometrically the birth of Horus (the sun, or monad of the world,) from the wedding of Osiris and Isis. It constitutes the chief element of the figure seen on the thrones of the Pharaohs, especially Memnon, the colossus of the Theban plain, which appears there to represent materially, a knot of love, but scientifically, the birth of Harmony out of the contending elements of Discord. The Vesica Piscis entered into the design of the structure of the central room in the great pyramid, and was connected with the entire train of Egyptian Masonry which that pyramid, internally and externally, embodied and comprised.

Pausamas takes notice of a promontory in Brasia, on which were placed three large hats; but he has not recorded whether they were emblematical of the Dioscori or the Corybantes: nor is it material to my argument to settle the probabilities that these fictitious deities were the same persons under different appellations, for the hats were in reality a representation of the triad. The breastplate of Agamemnon had for a device a three-headed serpent; and the Thracians buried three silver images as a charm to prevent the incursions of barbarians. On the three peaks of Mount Olivet, king Solomon, in his dotage, erected shrines to the infamous Phoenician triad, which was a personification of Murder—Lust—Hate; the center peak being occupied by the temple of Ashtaroth, the Paphian Venus, whose symbol was a white pyramid; and hence a subterranean adytum or crypt was excavated in the rock, precisely of that form, for the secret celebrations of the libidinous goddess. Even the virtues of eminent individuals gave occasion for the exercise of the same distinction, as in the case of Isocrates, to whom the Athenians erected a statue, in commendation of his Perseverance, Prudence, and Independence.

If we pass from the east to the west, we shall find the same system in active operation. The Celts and Goths had each their triads of deity; and the Lithuanians possessed a private triad of their own, consisting of Fire—Wod—Snake; and the Celtic Druids found the trinity in the mistletoe, because its leaves and berries were formed in clusters of three united in one stalk; and also, in the trefoil or shamrock leaf, which was in like manner an emblem of three in one. Religion was considered under a triple denomination, *viz.*, mythological—civil—philosophical; so universally did this principle display itself; and its tenets were based on three fundamental articles: reverence for the deity—abstaining from evil—courage in battle. The rule for the preservation of health was a triad consisting of Cheerfulness—Temperance—Exercise.

The Druids ascribed the origin of all things to three fountains: salt water—rain—springs. During the initiations, three hymns were chanted before the fire to the deity, called Trigaranos, the triple crane. The primary bards were called Plennydd — Alawn — Gwron, or, in other words, Light — Harmony — Energy. The hierophant of the mysteries was Math — Mengw — Rhuddlwmgawr, or Eiddic — Gôr — Coll; and so on through a number of triads, to the amount of some hundreds. It was engraved on their coins in the form of a bird—a boat—a man. The arrangement of classes, both in civil and religious polity, partook of the ternary form. Nothing could be transacted without a reference to this number. On solemn occasions, the processions were formed three times round the sacred enclosure of Caer Sidi; their invocations were thrice repeated; and even their poetry was composed in triads. The ternary deiseal, or procession from east to west by the south, accompanied all their rites, whether civil or ecclesiastical; and nothing was accounted sanctified without the performance of this preliminary ceremony. In a word, the triad formed the spirit of the Druidical religion; it was introduced into their poetry; it pervaded their philosophy, politics, and morals; and, like the property for which the number Three was venerated by all antiquity, it formed the beginning—middle—end of all their policy, whether civil, military, or religious.

Now how could it have been possible for all this uniformity to have arisen, except from some ancient tradition, which was universally received before the separation of the great family of mankind? The coincidence so widely disseminated could not be the effect of accident; and reason would never have discovered a doctrine so abstruse and difficult of comprehension that the wisest philosophers were divided in opinion whether to consider the triad as three separate deities, three hypostases, or merely three simple qualities of the same divine being. The correct knowledge which the ancient philosophers and sages possessed, was however admitted to be derived, and not discovered. And this is a most important distinction, which ought never to be lost sight of. Plato himself—the divine Plato, as his admirers styled him—speaks so very confusedly on this subject, that his followers were not agreed whether he admitted three or more hypostases into his theory of the divinity. And the style of reasoning adopted by his disciples abounds with such subtleties, that it is difficult to gather from their writings whether they themselves really understood their own arguments. Plato taught, according to Porphyry, that the divine essence may possibly extend itself to three hypostases, viz., the Supreme Divinity—the Creator—the Soul of the World. But in another place, he says, "We must not consider the Supreme Divinity as one of the hypostases, because he is incapable of accidents, and has no communication with any other being; and therefore, in considering the Divinity, we must begin with the Spirit or Creator." Hence Parmenidas, the Platonist, makes the deity not confining the hypostases to any specific number; although Plotinus, in his Enneades, explains the expression by affirming that he meant a triad of archical hypostases. But the same philosopher, in another place, asserts that the trinity consists of more than three hypostases; whom, however, Porphyry, his pupil, does not follow, but confines the triad to its legitimate number, in conformity with the ancient belief. Aurelius makes the trinity to consist of three equal *persons*; while Iamblichus, and a few of the later Platonists, endeavored in vain to extend the number of hypostases, and to exalt the first to a rank high above the rest.

Having thus shown that the knowledge of a triad of deity existed in the heathen world long before the birth of Plato, it will fully refute the assertion so boldly promulgated in these days, that the doctrine of the trinity was introduced into Christianity by Justin Martyr, who, before his conversion, was a Platonic philosopher.

The perversion of the primitive doctrine of the trinity before the coming of Christ was so complete, that the heathen philosophers "confessed unanimously that the sun is an emblem or image of the three great deities jointly and individually; that is, of Brahm, or the supreme one, who alone exists really and absolutely; the three small divinities being only Maya, or illusion." In another point of view, the triad was referred to the Triple oil spring of Noah, and it was dramatized in the Spurious Freemasonry, by the funereal ceremony of initiation; for, as the infernal regions consisted of three parts, Elysium—Purgatory—Tartarus, so the initiations were divided into three degrees, Preparation—Initiation—Autopsia. The preparation was also three-fold; so careful was the hierophant that a veneration for this sacred number should be inculcated in all the forms of initiation. The candidate was placed in the pastos on the evening of the first day; remained an entire day enclosed or dead, in the language of the Spurious Freemasonry, and was liberated for initiation, or in other words, restored to life on the third. And this ceremony produced a series of triad references. It was symbolical of Noah, who entered into the ark in one year, remained enclosed a year, and was emancipated from his confinement, or reborn, in the third year. Much confusion arose, in the mythology of the ancient world, from this doctrine. The aspirant, like Noah, is supposed to have lived in the old world, and was hence esteemed a venerable old man; but he was newborn from the mysteries, as Noah was from the ark, and hence he was considered but an infant. Noah formed the ark, and it was consequently represented as his *daughter*; but he was united with the ark, and hence she was taken for his *wife*; and ultimately, he was born from the ark, which from this circumstance sustained the character of his mother. Again, when he is said to die, the ark is his *coffin*; when a child, it is his *cradle*; and when he is supposed to sleep in deep repose during the prevalence of the waters, it is his bed. The confusion this would necessarily create, could not be reconciled without having recourse to a plurality of deities; and therefore in Greece, as the father of the female principle or ark, Noah was termed Saturn; as her husband, he was termed *Jupiter*; as her son, *Bacchus;* and when the solar and the arkite superstitions were connected, he became Apollo, and soon branched off into a number of collateral deities which peopled the imaginary heaven, and tended to mystify the system of religion, and place it entirely out of the reach of ordinary comprehension.

To wade further through this disgusting mass of absurdity and error will be unnecessary. Enough has been said to evince the fact that THREE was a number venerated by all nations; emanating, as it is not improbable, from the notion of a divine triad, which prevailed throughout the heathen world, with striking marks of uniformity amongst tribes which were separated from each other by such impassible barriers as to render it clear that the idea must have been derived from some remote tradition of a similar doctrine, which was prevalent and well understood when mankind dwelt together as one family. And this could be nothing but the doctrine of a trinity in unity. In process of time, the most absurd fancies respecting its use and application became engrafted on the naked doctrine, until it puzzled the wisest philosophers, who confounded the properties ascribed to the various persons, attributing them indiscriminately to either of the three forms of the sacred triad; and the true meaning was lost amidst the darkness and difficulty which surrounded the interpretation. The notion, however, of a triad resolving itself into a monad, how obscure soever it might be, was undoubtedly propagated; that being familiarized to the mind by the direction of an overruling Providence, mankind might be prepared to receive the true doctrine, when it should be propounded to them by authority, in that glorious dispensation, which, in God's good time, will constitute the universal religion of the whole habitable globe.

Hence we deduce the wisdom and utility of suffering this sublime doctrine,—vague and unsatisfactory as it appears to have been, in the degenerate form which it subsequently assumed in the several branches of Spurious Freemasonry which existed in different nations,—to constitute a part of all those systems of false worship which the pride, or ignorance, or folly of man's heart induced him to establish and practice, in the vain hope of rendering a service acceptable to the Deity, or of propitiating those imaginary beings whom vanity had elevated to the doubtful station of mediators between God and man. Nothing could have better served the purpose of making the revelation of Christianity acceptable to both Jews and heathen. They possessed indistinct notions of a trinity in unity, and anxiously awaited the explication of a doctrine which had been equally sublime and incomprehensible. That which had been impenetrable mystery was clearly explained at the incarnation of the Messiah; and the enlightened Gentile as well as the pious Jew, at once saw and acknowledged the propriety of a doctrine, which had formerly been to both a subject of confused theory and unsatisfactory speculation. "Come and see," exclaims the Rabbi Simeon Ben Jochai, in the Book of Zohar, as cited by Allix, "come and see the mystery in the word Elohim. There are three degrees, and every degree is distinct by himself; yet notwithstanding they are all one, and bound together in one, nor can they be separated each from the other."

I conclude, therefore, in the language of the late Bishop Tomline, "that nearly all the pagan nations of antiquity, in their various theological systems, acknowledged a kind of trinity in the divine nature, has been fully evinced by those learned men who have made the heathen mythology the subject of their elaborate inquiries. The almost universal prevalence of this doctrine in the Gentile kingdoms must be considered as a strong argument in favor of its truth. The doctrine itself bears such striking internal marks of a divine original, and is so very unlikely to have been the invention of mere human reason, that there is no way of accounting for the general adoption of so singular a belief, but by supposing that it was revealed by God to the early patriarchs, and that it was transmitted by them to their posterity. In its progress, indeed, to remote countries, and to distant generations, this belief became depraved and corrupted in the highest degree; and He alone, who brought life and immortality to light, could restore it to its original simplicity and purity. The discovery of the existence of this doctrine in the early ages, among the nations whose records have been the best preserved, has been of great service to the cause of Christianity, and completely refutes the assertion of infidels and sceptics, that the sublime and mysterious doctrine of the trinity owes its origin to the philosophers of Greece. If we extend our eye through the remote region of antiquity, we shall find this very doctrine, which the primitive Christians are said to have borrowed from the Platonic school, universally and immemorially flourishing in all those countries where history and tradition have united to fix those virtuous ancestors of the human race, who, for their distinguished attainments in piety, were admitted to a familiar intercourse with Jehovah, and the angels—the divine heralds of his commands."

The reflections arising from this subject are of the most awful and impressive nature. They should operate to throw us unreservedly on the mercy of the true trinity in unity, that we be not lost in the path of presumption on the one hand, or in that of infidelity on the other. They should strengthen our Faith, invigorate our Hope, and animate our CHARITY. Thus, will our grateful praises and thanksgivings ascend to the throne of grace, like the smoke of an evening sacrifice; and our piety and devotion be more acceptable than the richest incense of the altar. Three times will the Almighty visit the world in wrath. First, God the Father destroyed all created life, except a favored few, by a flood of waters, to punish the iniquities of men. Then a more awful manifestation took place. In the midst of justice remembering mercy, He accepted a substitute to appease his justly excited anger, in the person of his only begotten Son; who, when the atonement was made, commissioned the Holy Ghost to dwell in the hearts of men as a Comforter, that they might avoid the consequences of the third display of vengeance. Lastly, our planetary system will be dissolved by a terrific manifestation of the Trinity; our earth will become the prey of elemental fire, and condemned to wander forever a blazing comet through universal space, as a beacon to warn the creatures of other spheres how dreadful is the wrath of an offended God.

EVIDENCES, DOCTRINES, AND TRADITIONS

In the extreme west we find the Spurious Freemasonry celebrated, in like manner, in dark caverns of the earth valleys of the shadow of death—which still remain in all their native horror. "In Peru, numerous galleries built with stone, arid communicating with each other by shafts, fill up the interior of the artificial hills." Many of these excavations have been discovered in different parts of this continent. Two fine caves, resembling the extraordinary caverns in the Peak of Derbyshire, have recently been found about twelve miles from Albany. "I have been assured," says M. Humboldt, "by some Indians of Cholula, that the inside of the pyramids is hollow; and that, during the abode of Cortes in this city, their ancestors had concealed in the body of the pyramid, a considerable number of warriors, who were to fall suddenly on the Spaniards; but the materials of which the Teocalli is built, and the silence of the historians of those times, give but little probability to this latter assertion. It is certain, however, that in the interior of the pyramids there are considerable cavities, which were used as sepulchers, and for other purposes."

The use of these caverns by the Mexican hierophant has been thus described. The candidate descended into the dark and cheerless caverns which had been excavated beneath the foundations of the temple, and passed through the horrible mysteries of the Mexican religion, which emblematically represented the wanderings of their god. These caverns were denominated "the path of the dead," corresponding with "the place of souls" mentioned by Eustathius. Every step he took, some fearful object met his eyes, some appalling sound struck upon his ear; and he proceeded with measured pace, fearful lest the knife of the sacrificing priest should be applied to him; or that an incautious step might precipitate him into some deep and hidden pitfall, where his cries would not be heard. Thus, was he conducted through caverns slippery with half-congealed blood—damp, gloomy, and full of terror. His ears are saluted with heavy groans; his heart throbs as they seem to rise from beneath his feet; his fears are realized; for here lay the quivering frame of a dying victim, whose heart has been violently rent from its living sepulcher, and offered up in sacrifice to the sanguinary gods.

Hurried on from one horror to another, it was only the rapidity of his movements that prevented him from sinking under the trial; it was only the change of scene and situation, which, dissipating reflection, supported him under the arduous ceremony. At length, they arrived at a narrow chasm, or stone fissure, at the termination of this extensive range of caverns, through which the aspirant was formally protruded, and was received by a shouting multitude in the open air, as a person regenerated or born again.

It will be unnecessary to adduce any further proofs to establish the fact, that the holy mountain and the sacred valley of antiquity, used first by the patriarchs, and perverted by idolaters, were the original materials of the Masonic tradition, that "Our ancient Brethren held their Lodges on the highest of hills, or in the lowest of valleys."

The early Christians, during the hot persecutions to which they were frequently subjected, retired to these caves and recesses of the mountains, conformably to the advice of our Savior—Let them that be in Judea flee to the mountains and here they celebrated their rites in secrecy and seclusion. Thus, Fosbroke says: "The catacombs and crypts of the first Christians at Rome were originally excavations for finding puzzolana, supposed to form the best and most lasting cement. They followed the direction of the vein of sand, and were abandoned when they were exhausted, and oftentimes totally forgotten. Such lone unfrequented caverns afforded a most commodious retreat to the Christians, during the persecutions of the three first emperors. In them, therefore, they held their assemblies, celebrated the holy mysteries, and deposited the remains of their martyred brethren."

In speaking of the traditional hill and valley, it may be remarked, as connected in some degree with our subject, that bur Savior was born in one of these consecrated grottos or caverns. A belief was also prevalent amongst the early Christians, that his Second Advent would occur in the year 1000 of our era; and that the Valley of Jehosaphat, a deep ravine, without the city of Jerusalem, was to be the scene of the final judgment. Hence, pilgrimages from every part of Christendom became so very prevalent about that period, as to make some kind of institutions necessary for the protection of these pious devotees at a period when travellers were exposed to all sorts of dangers. This was the origin of the knightly orders. Hospitals were established for the entertainment of the pilgrims in health, and for their relief in sickness. In the above valley, the first and principal house was erected; and its benevolent inmates are reputed to have been, not only valiant knights, but also worthy Freemasons. The buildings were capacious, and a church was attached to them, dedicated to the Virgin Mary. During the first crusade, the knights' companions of these hospitals gained such celebrity by their valor in the field, and by their careful attendance on the sick and wounded soldiers of the Cross, that the gratitude of their leaders was unbounded. Kings, princes, and barons endowed them with lands and privileges; conferred on their houses a regular system of government; and the order of the Knights Hospitallers soon became famous, not only for offices of charity, but also as valiant men-at-arms.

Their fame and emoluments excited competition, and produced another order of military monks, whose fame was speedily extended to every quarter of the globe. The pilgrims were provided by the Hospitallers with food and refreshment at the several stages of their journey to the Valley of Jehosaphat. But these were necessarily placed at a very great distance from each other in the several countries of Europe and Asia; and in the intermediate spaces, the pilgrims were still exposed to many dangers, and needed protection. For this purpose, nine valiant knights—members of the Masonic Fraternity—formed themselves into a voluntary society, vowing to live a life of celibacy, to have a stated residence near the Holy Sepulcher, and to be always on the alert to defend pilgrims against the machinations of Jews, Turks, infidels, and heretics. They bound themselves by the usual monastic vows, and erected their domicile near the precincts of the Holy Temple. This was the origin of the Templars. As the Hospitallers held their secret conclaves in the deep Valley of Jehosaphat, so the Templars assembled in an encampment on the summit of Moriah. And thus, these primitive warrior Masons met "on the highest of hills, and in the lowest of valleys."

Is it contended that the circumstances which rendered such precautions necessary, would operate unfavorably to the spread of truth? The fact is freely admitted. They would have a tendency to operate unfavorably. In a dark and superstitious age, secrets and mystery were objects of suspicion; and the purity of their characters would not remove the jealousy with which the fraternity was regarded. Indeed, if we refer to a much later period—even to the middle ages of Christianity—when our cathedrals and collegiate churches were springing up in all their majesty throughout Christendom; the builders, whose plans and designs were perfected within secret conclaves, frequently holden in the concealed crypts beneath the sacred edifice—a type of the original valley—and which were probably constructed for that very purpose, were reputed to possess knowledge and power which were unattainable by human means. And it is true, that they were the masters of a science beyond the acquisition of other men. Nor did the avowal, that it had been attained by intense study and application, abate the suspicion with which their secret meetings were regarded. Men are always jealous of those who have outstripped them in the walks of science and learning. Envy is a powerful affection of the mind; and, as has been beautifully observed, attends upon merit as its shadow. The master-mind which governs and directs the will of others at his pleasure, must expect detraction, as the price of his superiority. And slander and detraction are opposed to the principles of Freemasonry. But it was not the Freemason who practiced it. It was the cowan who envied him; and it did operate unfavorably, even in the face of his immortal productions.

But the cautious secrecy of the Craft in those ages, was used to prevent the great principles of science, by which their reputation was secured and maintained, from being publicly known. Even the workmen—the E. A.P.'s—the F.C.'s, were unacquainted with the secret and refined mechanism which cemented and imparted the treasures of wisdom. They were profoundly ignorant of the *wisdom* which planned—the *beauty* which designed—and knew only the *strength* and labor which executed the work. The doctrine of the pressure and counter-pressure of complicated arches was a mystery which they never attempted to penetrate. They were blind instruments in the hands of intelligent Master Masons, and completed the most sublime undertakings by the effect of mere mechanical skill and physical power; without being able to comprehend the secret which produced them; without understanding the nice adjustment of the members of a building to each other, so necessary to accomplish a striking and permanent effect: or without being able to enter into the science exhibited in the complicated details which were necessary to form a harmonious and proportionate whole.

The masters of the work were thus figuratively said to form their Lodges on the highest of hills, or in the lowest of valleys, that they might enter—without fear of interruption, from the jealousy of the people on the one hand, or the curiosity of the more ambitious fellow-crafts on the other—on those abstruse calculations which were necessary to carry on the work with credit to themselves, and advantage to their employers; and to complete the drawings on their several tracing-boards, that they might be distributed amongst the workmen, according to their several stations, when they returned from refreshment to labor. Few were admitted to the highest grade of the order, and those after a long and severe probation under the Master's eye, and on the establishment of unexceptionable proofs of moral, as well as scientific excellence. To these, the Master's Lodge was at length open, and all the abstruse secrets of the order fully unveiled.

By such means a succession of Rulers was provided, who brought down Operative Masonry, improved in beauty and magnificence, to a time when public prejudice was overcome, and the brethren were honored by the noble, the wealthy, and the wise. From this period regularly-formed Lodges were universally adopted; the meetings on hills and in valleys ceased; and the Masons of the present day are unacquainted with the custom, except as it is viewed through the long vista of forgotten ages; or its inconveniences contemplated through the medium of Masonic tradition.

I shall conclude this paper with a few observations on this symbol:

which some consider to mean Templum Riero-solvmae, others refer it to the Phallus, and others to the Nilometre, or key of the river Nile. I consider it to be an emblem of Christian Freemasonry. The signs or marks of our sublime science are generally explained on a principle which is evident and satisfactory, and not liable to misapprehension. Whether these symbols have been constructed from instruments of manual labor,—from geometrical figures,—from the works of nature,—or the sublime vaults of Heaven,—there can be no doubt in the well-instructed Mason's mind, respecting their general reference and application. The design of their adoption was to embody valuable moral and religious truths, that the view of a sensible object might raise before the contemplative brother's mental eye, some intellectual maxim, by which he might become wiser and better. This is, indeed, a noble design. It allures to the pursuit of virtue, and inspires a love for investigations whose aim and end are the perfection of our mental faculties. And thus, science is applied to the practice of moral virtue and religious duty.

The fraternity does not appear to be agreed respecting the Masonic mark, or emblem, to which I have just alluded. Its interpretation has been involved in mystery. Nor do the general discussions which prevail amongst the Brethren tend to elucidate the subject in a manner that is perfectly satisfactory. The Tau Cross **T**, which distinguishes the Master Mason's apron, has been referred to the Three Great Lights of Masonry, which represent the Sacred Word, expressive of his creative, preserving, and destroying power. These lights are placed in the form of an equilateral triangle, each of the lesser intersecting the line formed by the two greater. Thus, geometrically dividing the greater triangle into three lesser triangles, at its extremities; and by their union, form a fourth triangle in the center; all of them being equal and equilateral; emblematical equally of the Tetragrammaton and the Four Degrees of Masonry. This symbolical arrangement appears to correspond with the mysterious Tau dross triplified, which forms two right angles on each of the exterior lines, and another at the center by their union; for the three angles of each triangle are equal to two right angles. This illustrates the jewel worn by the Companions of the R. A., which, by its intersection, forms a given number of angles. These may be taken in five several combinations; and being reduced, their amount in right angles will be found equal to the five Platonic bodies, which represent the four elements and sphere of the universe. But this has been deemed no satisfactory explanation of the precise meaning of the symbol.

The letter Tau is translated from the Chaldaic Hebrew, to signify the mark or sign spoken of by the angel, which Ezekiel saw in the spirit, when the man with the writer's inkhorn was recommended to go through the cities of Jerusalem, and set the mark of God on those who sigh and cry for the abominations that are done in the midst thereof. And by this mark they were preserved when, by the wrathful displeasure of Jehovah, the idolatrous people were slain. Hence, in ancient times, this mark T was set on those who had been acquitted by their judges, in token of their innocence. The military commanders placed it on those who escaped unhurt from the field of battle, as a symbol of safety under the divine protection. For these causes, it has been designated an emblem of LIFE. And in our own island, it was highly venerated in connection with the oak, which was a tree sacred amongst all nations, and considered as peculiarly sanctified by the gods, if not their immediate residence. The fairest tree in the grove was solemnly consecrated with many superstitious ceremonies: Sometimes it was divested of some of its collateral branches, and one of the largest was preserved, and so constructed as to exhibit the form of the Tau Cross. On the back of the tree they inscribed the word Tau, by which, says Borlase, they meant God. On the right arm was inscribed Hesus, on the left, Belenus, and on the middle of the trunk, Tharamis. This was to represent the sacred triad. It is rather curious, and displays the workings of an overruling Providence, that the Jews and Romans should have condemned Jesus to die by the very instrument which, in all nations, had been previously esteemed the symbol of *eternal life*. And hence it appears that this emblem T amongst Christians, was not altogether primitive. But it is by no means clear that the early converts were acquainted with its use amongst their heathen neighbors; although at Rome the statue of Osiris was distinguished by it; and in Egypt the same figure was sculptured on gems, and signified *vitam eternam*. And when the Temple of Osiris, at Alexandria, was destroyed at the command of Theodosius, crosses were found cut in stone, which, as we are informed by Socrates, occasioned many of the people to become Christians. "The sign of the cross," says Edmonstone, "amongst the Egyptians, signified Life; and was the mark by which they expressed the number Ten, which was a perfect number, denoting Heaven, and the Pythagorean Tetractys, or incommunicable Name of God." The symbolical pagan cress was originally the Tautic, not the compound figure with four arms ✚; for this last, I apprehend, was more modem than the former, being, in fact, merely a double T.

This symbol, as I have already observed, is interpreted by some of our Brethren to allude to the temple at Jerusalem, (Templum Hierosolymae), who think that the T is placed over the H to denote the superiority of the place which was the habitation of God, over that which was only the dwelling-place of man; for though the city was holy, the temple exceeded it in holiness. Others consider it, I apprehend with greater reason, to be the Tau Cross of heathen nations triplified. <u>Count de Gebelin</u> **(Initiated the interpretation of the Tarot as an arcane repository of timeless esoteric wisdom in 1781)** informs us, that this symbol T was carried by the Egyptian priests during the processions attending their most sacred rites; and therefore, was not unknown to the Israelites in their wanderings, and was consequently a Jewish emblem in existence before the Temple of Solomon was erected. It is, indeed, inserted as a sacred symbol on the Isiac Table; and hence, has been taken by some for a Nilometre, or key of the Nile, to measure the increase and decrease of its fructifying waters. This latter opinion is, I am persuaded, erroneous; for the Nilometre would scarcely have been considered of sufficient importance to be stamped on the forehead of the Egyptian <u>Epopts</u> **(An initiate in the Eleusinian Mysteries)**: nor could it have been imitated in Persia 5 and the Tau, as Tertullian informs us, (and he is an unexceptionable authority, because he had himself been initiated before his conversion to Christianity), was inscribed on the forehead of every person who had been admitted into the mysteries of Mithras.

Other opinions have been delivered, which it would be improper to introduce here.

How true soever it may be that the Tau Cross was used by the Hebrews before their deliverance from Egyptian bondage, and continued through the entire period of their history, I shall treat it, in its triplifical character ⊓⊓, as a symbol peculiarly adapted to Christian Freemasonry; thus partaking of the typical nature and application of all other parts of the Jewish mode of worship; for although the single Tail Cross is found amongst the symbols of many ancient nations, we have no certain evidence that the Triple Tau, combined in this form, as an angle symbol, existed till after the Crucifixion of Christ And I am inclined to think, that it was adopted in some very early age of the church, as a monogram to represent the Great I A M, by whom the gloomy and shapeless masses of chaos were changed into order, regularity, and beauty, and probably used as the sign or mark of some eminent ecclesiastical architect, and thence perpetuated in the system of Freemasonry as a Master's Mark; for it is the precise form which was anciently termed the Greek Cross. And thus, we find it represented on coins.

Of one of the coins on which this symbol appears, Dr. Walsh writes thus: "Justinian erected a statue in the Augusteion, to which he gave the globe and cross which others had confined to their coins. He seemed ambitious of distinction in minor points. He modified the form of the cross into that which still continues in the eastern church to be peculiarly called the Greek Cross; and he bent down the tiara, so as to give it the shape of the modern crown surmounted by a cross, as used at present by Christian monarchs. These circumstances are commemorated on his coins. The above represents the Greek Cross standing on a pedestal of steps."

EVIDENCES, DOCTRINES, AND TRADITIONS

INFLUENCE ON THE MORAL AND SOCIAL CONDITION OF MAN

Freemasonry is a comprehensive, which embraces all mankind in a common bond of universal brotherhood. Creeds or modes of faith are not allowed to interfere with or destroy its genial operation. All men are brethren. Those who are not Masons, lie under the general obligation to act at brethren to us, and to each other, as we do to all the world, and in particular to those of our pious and honorable community. For by creation, we are all the children of one common parent; of one blood, the Great Architect of the World made all the families of the earth. See the order of his work: he laid the broad foundation of the universe; he raised, without axe or hammer, the circular walls of this terraqueous globe; he roofed it with yonder beautiful canopy, and ornamented it with all those unnumbered and unmeasurable glittering orbs of shining light and luster; perfected it in all its beauty, and furnished it with all its utility; and, like a workman who needeth not to be ashamed of his performance, pronounced the wondrous fabric good, perfect, and complete. Next, be built the human frame, and furnished it with immortality; pronounced his creature man very good; sent him forth as an inhabitant of his new-made world; bid him multiply; and declared him the common father of the intended human race. From this stock, all mankind was propagated—ALL ARE BRETHREN; Adam was our federal head, and Adam was the son of God.

As, therefore, all men bear the same Relation to each other,

Freemasonry, which professes to convey benefits to all ranks and descriptions of men, extends her arms of love and charity to the inhabitant of the earth, without, reference to birth, language, education, or the color of the skin; male and female, infancy, manhood, and old age—all are included in its universal bond; and all, I am inclined to believe, participate in its blessings. It is true the benefits derived by the uninitiated are less obvious, because they refuse to acknowledge them; but still they do partake, to a certain extent, in the unalloyed good which is distributed throughout society by the prevailing, though secret influence of masonry, to promote its moral and social interests.

Our Rev. Bro. Town says, "when we speak of the moral principles of Freemasonry, we mean such as emanate from the divine essence, and immutable perfections of God. Such as impress their own truth, and carry conviction of a just sense of duty to every enlightened conscience; such as arc perfectly adapted to the constitutional endowments of man as an intellectual, moral, and social being, and especially such as the understanding will at once perceive to involve his highest and best interests, both as a creature of time, and an heir of immortality. In this, we are not to be understood as saying that the masonic code embodies every distinctive principle of moral virtue, in its more expanded form, but only such as may be brought to bear on a specific object of common interest, and *in the best manner subserve the accomplishment of a special purpose connected with the happiness of all our species.*"

This proposition, which every thinking Mason will be able to verify, and none will venture to dispute, is still doubted by some of our opponents amongst the uninitiated and denied by others. And it is most extraordinary, that men of talent, who are professedly ignorant of the true design of Masonry, should compromise their reputation by writing on a subject where the information is sure to be superficial and imperfect, because it is derived from false lights, which always lead the enquirer into error. And it is seldom that our foes will take the trouble of reading any authorized work on

Masonry, lest, perhaps, they should be enlightened, and cease to be opponents. Such uncandid persons commence their hospitality by retailing slander, and throwing out insinuations at clubs and private coteries, which are generally well received, because such assemblies are congregated for amusement only, and require nothing but racy anecdotes, true or untrue, to promote the exhilaration of the present moment. A rolling snowball rapidly increases in magnitude, and so does an unfounded report. The debutant, proud of his applause, widens the circle of its charges against the Order; and his popularity increases in proportion as they become more improbable and mysterious. Finding, greatly to his astonishment, that he has become, not only "a hero of dinner tables," but also "the pet of the drawing room", by denouncing an institution which excludes females from its secret celebrations; he at length determines to write, and thus seal the perpetuity of his fame. This, I believe, will be a correct description of the usual progress which has distinguished the career of all the adversaries of Freemasons.

"The charges which pertness, flippancy, and bigotry, prefer against us," as the Chevalier Adamo once observed in a speech at a festival of Lodge 50, in Dublin, "I disdain to meet; but if any man in a spirit of sober investigation, seeks to know in what Masonry consists, I tell him that it venerates and honors religion; I tell him it prohibits intemperance, inculcates order, honesty, sobriety, decorum—that it enjoins the practice of abstemiousness, sincerity, and universal benevolence. If he says this is a vague assertion, I will convince him by facts. I will take him to the house of mourning, where the widow weeps hopelessly over her desolate children—where penury and want have made their abode—where the silence of despair is only broken by the sigh of the broken-hearted orphan, I will show him the benevolent spirit of our institution, entering the abode of wretchedness, presenting the masonic cup of consolation to the widow, assuring her of protection, and the orphan of support. But while the objects of our peculiar care are the members of our own confraternity, whom poverty and misfortune have prostrated in the dust, *there is nothing selfish in the charity we profess, for we are enjoined in the practice of universal benevolence.* I may be told that every Christian may do as much; I answer, yes, he *ought*,—but a Mason *must*."

Such testimonies, from such men, must be sufficient, if candidly considered, to disarm this malignity, and make them friendly to the Order. Should it fail, there is no remedy but the infliction of that curious punishment which we find described in an ancient writer, as a slight memento to those unfortunate persons who dogmatically presumed to dictate to others what they did not understand themselves; it was to this effect. A certain witty rake, called Muthodes, was much given to slander, and entertained his friends, at their symposiacs, with anecdotes that were invented for the occasion, and strictures on various sciences of which he was known to be notoriously ignorant. At length, he began to meddle with the affairs of state, condemning all the wine and benevolent institution of antiquity. Intelligence of this being conveyed to the Archon, he caused the two tall stakes to be placed perpendicularly in the ground, and a third laid horizontally across the top; and commanded that the culprit should be suspended by the heels from the center of the machine; this being considered the proper position of those who willfully misrepresent facts, and turn the truth upside down. The unauthorized words which Muthodes had been guilt; of using, were then fairly transcribed, each on a separate piece of paper, and being rolled up into pellets, were enclosed in the leaf of a cabbage, and he was compelled to swallow them in detail, one by one, till all were consumed. Now the cabbage being esteemed a sovereign antidote against drunkenness, it was prescribed in this case, because the man who pretends to give an opinion on a subject which he does not understand, is guilty of willful falsehood—and willful falsehood is a species of moral intoxication. And, as a further precaution against a renewal of the offense, the delinquent was placed in an inverted posture, that the fumes of the indigestible verbiage might rise into the epigastrium, and the brain remain untouched. This was considered to be a never-falling cure for the complaint.

INFLUENCE ON THE MORAL AND SOCIAL CONDITION OF MAN

Our opponents will perhaps be gratified to learn, how reluctant soever they may be to admit the fact, in what manner the influence of Masonry operates; because, they may probably think, that as its effects do not always appear on the surface, and the institution does not obtrude itself on public notice by the use of such means as are resorted to by some other societies, to secure the applause of the multitude, its moral efficacy is questionable. I am ready to admit, that Freemasonry is of a retiring character; that it distributes its benefits noiselessly, and does not let its left band know what its right hand doeth. But its influence on society is not the less certain, nor its benefits the less operative, on that account. And I shall endeavor to demonstrate this proportion by showing, that Freemasonry actually recommends all those virtues, and forbids all those vices, which tend to promote or retard the welfare of civil society; and that the example of its members imparts a silent lesson, which, though it may not be obvious to the sight, works secretly for the benefit of the toe community at lane.

And first it will be observed, that influence is of two kinds, direct and indirect. The first embraces precept and example, the second may be subdivided into positive and negative. These I shall consider seriatim **(Taking one subject after another in regular order; point by point)**; and I flatter myself that I shall convince the reader—as I am myself convinced—that Freemasonry possesses a considerable influence on the moral and social condition of man, however it may be overlooked by the thoughtless, doubted by the sceptic, or dented by those who regard our proceedings with envy and ill-will.

All such persons, from what cause soever their hostility may arise, in their ignorance of our practices, expose themselves in mass, by contradicting and refuting each other's theory. One wittily accuses us of practicing an institution which is out of the pale of Christianity; another condemns us because, as he says, we make it a Christian institution, and endeavor to pass it off as a substitute for the gospel. How can these two adversaries reconcile the grounds of their hostility to tile Order, when neither of them can tell which is right and which is wrong? There are many other anomalies into which these critics fall and ensnare themselves, when they plunge into a stream whose depth has not been sounded. Our transgressions, according to the evidence of these worthies, are too numerous to be either overlooked or forgiven. Freemasonry is frivolous and absurd—it is useless—it is unsocial—it is anti-monarchial—it is an emanation of paganism—it imposes unlawful oaths—it is a spirit raising, gold making, fortune telling deception, exuded from the dross and filth of Rosicrucianism, &c &c. But the exclusion of females appears to be the _pons asinrrum_ **(the point at which many learners fail, especially a theory or formula that is difficult to grasp)** of the objectors. And he must be an adventurous knight, indeed, and clad _cap-a-pie_ **(From head to foot)** in armor of proof, who will venture to set his foot on unknown regions which lie beyond that forbidden barrier.

It is really a pity that any person of talent should please himself so completely under the dominion of prejudice, as to decry an institution which, at least, does no injury, even supposing that it does no good, which, however, I can by no means admit; for I consider it—and ever have considered it—the very first of human institutions; the dispenser of earthly blessings; because, as a masonic writer of the last century properly remarks—"It comprehends within its circle every branch of useful knowledge and learning, and stamps an indelible mark of preeminence on its genuine professors, which neither chance, power, nor fortune can bestow. When its rules are strictly observed, it is a sure foundation of tranquility amid the various disappointments of life; friend that will not deceive, but will comfort and assist, in prosperity and adversity; a blessing that will remain with all times, circumstances, and places; and to which recourse may be had, when other earthly comforts sink into disregard. And more than this, it gives real and intrinsic excellency to man, and renders him fit for the duties of society. It strengthens the mind against the storms of life, paves the way to peace, and promotes domestic happiness. It meliorates the temper and improves the understanding; it is company in solitude, and gives vivacity, variety, and energy, to social conversation. In youth, it governs the passions, and employs usefully our most active faculties; and in age when sickness, imbecility, and disease, have benumbed the corporeal frame, and rendered the union of soul and body almost intolerable, it yields an ample fund of comfort and satisfaction."

Under these circumstances I may be asked, as I frequently have been, why I give myself the trouble to enlighten the understanding of men who have eyes, but will not see; who have ears, but will not hear; and who have comprehension, but will not understand? It is a posing question, and can only be answered, by saying with the indifferent sportsman, that when he shoots into the midst of a flock of gulls, he sometimes, by chance, brings down a bird. So, in these strictures I may succeed in opening the eyes of an occasional gainsayer to the truth, and show him what a gull he has been by giving implicit credit to crude assertions unaccompanied by proof. Besides, there is always a suspicion on the slanderer, which frequently turns his defamation against Himself; and a very few words of vindication will often be sufficient to neutralize whole volumes of abuse. I once knew a schoolmaster who bestowed great pains to persuade his pupils of the moral turpitude of Freemasonry. And his denunciations of the institution were pompous and incessant. But the pedagogue overshot his mark; the suspicions of the boys were aroused, and when they were emancipated from fears of the birch, and became men, most of them sought initiation that they might ascertain the correctness of the hypothesis, and be enabled practically to refute the malicious insinuations which they had heard. And they entered with greater zeal into the practice of the Order, because they found good where they were instructed to expect evil.

All mankind is inclined to be captious, and to doubt the genial operation of what they do not perfectly understand. How else are we to account for the existence of all the absurd opinions which are afloat, respecting the means of salvation, and particularly for infidelity and atheism. The infidel will object as strongly against Christianity as the caviler does against Masonry. Yet they both continue their walk of benevolence and charity, undisturbed by the passing slander, which makes no more impression on either than the waft of an insect's wing would make of the gigantic oak. Persecution has always strengthened the cause it would destroy; and new attacks are but the harbingers of renewed prosperity. Freemasonry, the handmaiden of religion, is, in our own times, menaced by religious professors, which will prove an effectual antidote to Luke warmness on the one hand, and neglect on the other; and the Order is sure to derive essential benefits from every attack.

CHAPTER II

It will be perceived that the doctrines of Masonry are not only calculated to promote the happiness of this world, but extend also to the next if their influence were directed solely to the welfare of the body, and the soul left to the effect of chance, then their utility might be esteemed doubtful by those who are unacquainted with their real excellence. But this is not the case. The interests of both proceed by equal steps, and I am not aware that those of either were intended by the Supreme Architect of the Universe to operate independently of the other. The duties which we owe to God and to ourselves, run in the gospel in two parallel lines, and both contribute an equal share to the great end of our creation. "The full manifestation of that dominion," according to Archbishop Seeker, "which Christ in his human nature acquired, by dying, and rising, and living again (for which manifestation every other act of his regal authority is opening the way), will be in that hour when he shall come with his holy angels to sit upon the throne of his glory, and all nations being gathered before him, shall sentence the wicked to everlasting punishment, but bestow on the righteous life eternal. After which, the ends of this whole dispensation being now accomplished, he shall deliver up his kingdom of grace to God, even the Father, in whose kingdom of glory be shall still reign, with Him and the Holy Spirit, over his saints and angels forever."

AS MASONS we are bound by our obligation to contribute our share to this glorious consummation, by yielding a due obedience to the precepts of the Order, and exemplifying in our lives the lessons which are delivered in the lodge. So far, the Mason is in advance of the Christian, because he not only enjoys the advantages of Christian teaching in common with every other person, but also hears those vivifying precepts of Freemasonry, which, if he receives with meekness, and observes with fidelity, will bring him to "a building not made with hands, eternal in the heavens." That this proposition may receive every confirmation of which it is susceptible, I propose, in these papers, to give an outline of the instruction which distinguishes a Masons lodge, for the purpose of showing that while the Mason, by the practice of Christianity is working out his own salvation, he is at the same time, by the practice of Masonry, contributing, in no slight degree, to the general interests of society.

I have said in a former chapter, that influence is neither direct nor indirect; and operates by precept and example. Direct influence is professedly applied by Freemasonry to the community at large with the avowed purpose of proving a genial effect on the morale of the people; and is displayed in those valuable publications on the subject, which have received the sanction and patronage of successive Grand Masters, and are considered to contain the fundamental principles of the Order. These books are open to the inspection of the public; and their operation is by no means equivocal. It is not to be believed that they are read only by Masons, and that uninitiated persons feel no interest in their perusal. They are read more universally than is generally supposed, and the effect they have produced are not hidden under a bushel. A comparison between the public feeling with regard to Freemasonry in the eighteenth and nineteenth centuries, will place this result in a clear and intelligible light.

In the eighteenth century, Freemasonry was regarded with great suspicion. It was believed to be a vehicle for the inculcation of principles which were opposed to human happiness and the general welfare of society. Some thought it a system of alchemy and superstition—others pronounced it to be concealed atheism or infidelity—some supposed it to be political and revolutionary—while others, more indulgent, considered it to be a mere convivial society, which afforded materials for spending a social evening with a company of known friends but all pronounced it to be useless—a waste of time—and an insult to the softer sex—of that sex which Ledyard, the universal traveller, justly says, are "in all countries civil, obliging, tender, and humane." And he adds, that "in wandering over the barren plains of inhospitable Denmark, through honest Sweden, frozen Lapland, rude and churlish Finland, and the widespread regions of the wandering Tartar; if hungry, dry, cold, wet, or sick, the women have ever been friendly to me, and uniformly so; and to add to this virtue, so worthy of the appellation of benevolence, these actions have been performed in so free and so kind a manner, that if I was thirsty, I drank the sweetest draught; and if hungry, I ate the coarsest food with a double relish." This confession is highly honorable to the sex, and is, in fact, the exercise of practical Freemasonry.

At the present time, a radical change has taken place in public opinion on the merits of Freemasonry, which has been produced chiefly through the influence of masonic publications. The Order is no longer proscribed as a baleful institution, unproductive of useful fruits; nor is it believed to be either infidel, superstitious, political, or revolutionary. Its public administrations are attended freely by all classes of people—its members enjoy the respect of the public—and its influence is allowed freely to operate for the general benefit of the community.

The second point proposed for our consideration is example; which, being publicly enunciated by the fraternity, is calculated,

INFLUENCE ON THE MORAL AND SOCIAL CONDITION OF MAN

by its influence to produce the most salutary effects on society at large; thus showing, in a striking point of view, the essential benefits which it derives from the operation of Freemasonry. Example is all powerful in virtue or in vice. The human mind is weak and unstable, and man, being an imitative animal, is easily led away by appearances. How very essential it is, then, that those appearances should range themselves on the aide of virtue. As the parent is, so will the child become. The servant will be like his master; and those who occupy the superior ranks of life will always lead their inferiors to good or evil. Here, then, we see the advantages that society derives from the beneficent example of Masons in their brotherly love—their mutual assistance—their support of each other in prosperity and adversity, in trouble and in joy.

This argument is too obvious to be overlooked, too apparent to be neglected, too valuable to be despised. From our example, the world may learn what great ends may be accomplished where a body of men unites, heart and hand, to promote a beneficent object. Accordingly, our charitable institutions are numerous and effective, for charity Forms the basis of our glorious Order.

There was an excellent custom in Lincolnshire some years ago—and I regret much that it has been discontinued, although it affords me great pleasure to reflect that it is still practiced in many other provinces—which had the effect of promoting the general interests of morality and religion through the influence of masonic example. I need not say that I refer to the annual custom of assembling all the lodges in the province alternately at the principal towns, and going in public procession to church, for the purpose of displaying a sense of gratitude and piety to God by offering up mutual prayers and thanksgiving, and advocating the cause of virtue and benevolence by an exposition from the pulpit on some of the numerous moral subjects which distinguishes the private lectures of the lodge. This custom brought the brethren into periodical communication with each other, and not only cemented old friendships, but formed new ones; thus extending the county acquaintance, and promoting brotherly love and social feeling amongst those, who might have remained strangers with each other till the day of their death; which is no slight advantage, because nothing can serve more strongly to cement the sacred ties of morality and virtue, than such an interchange of fraternal affection and goodwill. Besides, this admirable custom frequently generates a friendship which becomes mutually beneficial: old acquaintances are enabled to meet and renew those courtesies which time and distance had thrown into abeyance; and on such occasions, the heart and the tongue were found, as our motto predicates, to unite in promoting each other's welfare, and rejoice in each other's prosperity.

The exclusion of females from such celebrations has been considered the pet objection against the sociality of the Order; it may not therefore be amiss to observe in this place, that the argument is extended beyond its intimate application. It is well known that on all public occasions, ladies are admitted to the ceremonial; and in ancient times, it was customary to present distinguished females with roses and gloves, as a delicate compliment to their innocence and purity. In 1845, a remarkable instance of this custom occurred at a grand re-union and festival of the masonic Order at Kingston, Canada, where the emblematical rose and gloves were presented to several ladies; and to show the real estimation with which Freemasonry clothes the female character, I subjoin, from the report in Moore's Magazine, the address which was made when Mrs. Mackenzie Frazer was introduced on the platform. "The Worshipful Master descended from the throne, and said—High-born and excellent lady, the brethren of the most ancient of all societies, who, while they pursue in silence and seclusion the unvarying tenor of their way, forget not the claims of your sex for a single moment; and looking to the approval of woman as a guiding star, feel themselves peculiarly gratified in seeing you within this mystic circle of Freemasons, whose hearts are ever open and ever ready to acknowledge that to woman alone man owes the brightest portions of his character and his felicity. In the name of Solomon, I present you, lady, with the rose of beauty, and the spotless white gloves of innocence. Wear both, for of both are you worthy." And Colonel Mackenzie Frazer, on the part of Mrs. P., briefly replied; "and the rose of beauty and gloves of innocence were placed upon a pedestal, covered with a beautifully embroidered white satin cloth, and the oldest Mason offered them on a crimson velvet cushion." After this, let no one say that Masons neglect to pay due honor to female virtue and excellence.

The public observes with great curiosity all these reciprocal acts of mutual love and esteem, and prize them accordingly. And as example is better even than precept, they will endeavor to imitate them, each in his own circle of acquaintance; and thus, Freemasonry becomes a vehicle of incalculable benefit to those who have not received initiation into its mysteries.

What was said of the early Christians may be also said of us.— "It is inconceivable what unremitting diligence the Christians use to succor one another, since they have abandoned our religion (these are the words of a pagan writer) to adore a crucified man. Their teachers have acquired the wonderful art of persuading them that they are all brothers, insomuch that the whole of their possessions are given up for the general welfare. Nothing has contributed more to the progress of the Christian superstition than their attention to the poor and friendless; for they have hospital and asylums for indigence and infirmity in every city; and it is no small ground of reproach to us, that we should be so glaringly deficient in these things, whilst the Galileans cherish and relieve not only the wretched of their own communion, but likewise of ours."

A remarkable peculiarity of Freemasonry is that it does not court popularity; which may be one reason why it has become so highly esteemed in modern times. All our proceedings are carried on with the simple and exclusive design of working out its principles for our own mental improvement and happiness, both temporal and eternal, "We trace wisdom and follow virtue," that we may be happy ourselves and communicate happiness to others; but with no end in view, which is connected with the applause of men.

We aim at the cultivation of peace and harmony—peace on earth, and goodwill towards men—nor our progress in their attainment is marked and attested by the flourishing state of our lodges, and the respect, which is universally conceded, as if by common consent, to the name and character of a Mason.

We look upon ourselves as one great family, however we may be diversified by climate, education, or religion which makes no difference in the application of our principles, united as we are by an indissoluble bond to promote the welfare of each other, and associated for the noble purpose of improving the moral and social condition of mankind. And in this place, I cannot resist the impulse of quoting a passage from the Suffolk Rector's "Stray Leaves," it applies too well to the subject in hand.—The members of a Freemasons' lodge had solicited the Rev. Mr. Gresham for the use of his church for an anniversary sermon. After many objections on his part had been ably refuted by the dentation, he at length said—"I am hostile to you because you *combine*."

The banker now fired his broadside—"We do. We are as a city at unity in itself. We form a band of united brethren; bound by one solemn obligation, stringent upon all, from the highest to the lowest. And the object of our combination? boundless charity and untiring benevolence. We must be charitable and kindly affected to all, but more especially to our brethren. With them we are ever to sympathize readily, and their necessities to succor cheerfully. Respect are we to have none, either as to color, creed, or country. And yet is our charity to be neither indiscriminate, wasteful, nor heedless. We are to prefer the worthy brother, and to reject the worthless. And our warrant for so doing is His command who has said, 'thou shalt open thine hand wide to thy brother, and to the poor, and to the needy in thy land."

"The latter remark none can gainsay," said the vicar coldly; "and thus, I believe, our interview terminates."

The deputation retired, desperately chagrined. The church was closed against them. The new lodge was opened, but there was no public procession and no sermon. To me, lightly and carelessly, as I then thought of the fraternity, there seemed much that was inexplicable in the rebuff which it sustained. Here was Mr. Gresham, a conscientious and well-intentioned man, who lamented Sunday after Sunday, the prevalence of his sorrow, care, and suffering around him; who spoke, with tears in his eyes, of the apathy of the rich and the endurance of the poor; who deplored the selfishness of the age; who averred, bitterly and repeatedly, that *all sought their own*—here was he, withstanding to his utmost a brotherhood who declared, and none contradicted them, that their leading object was to relieve distress and sorrow. Of him, they seek an audience; when gained, they use it to request the use of his pulpit, with a view of making their principles better known; of effacing some erroneous impressions afloat respecting them; in other words, of strengthening their cause.

That cause they maintain to be identical with disinterested benevolence and brotherly love.

And shall such a cause remain any longer a doubtful question of right and wrong. "Shall its light be hidden under a bushel? Or shall that glorious moral force which, like the sun in the firmament of heaven enlightens and invigorates the nations of the earth—shall the real source of that noble principle by which society is so highly exalted in our own times, still remain concealed—or shall its light shine before men lo the glory of our Father which is in heaven?" These observations will aptly apply to the Masonry of the eighteenth century; and the same may be said of the fraternity as was said by heathen nations about the primitive Christians—"See how these Masons love another!"

CHAPTER III

It is an axiom universally admitted, that the practice of moral and social virtue will conduce to the promotion of human happiness. Whatever, therefore, has a tendency to enforce such a practice, will be entitled to the praise of conferring essential benefits on mankind. And that this is true with respect to Freemasonry, it will be my next business to prove.

In order to preserve society in a healthful state, it is necessary that regularity and order be strictly enforced by a due observance of the laws, without which, confusion and debauchery of every baleful kind would soon be introduced, to the destruction of that peace and harmony which arc blended in the details of masonic government, as being absolutely required to produce the comfort and happiness of its members, and the general well-being of the institution. The same may be said of the community at large. Courtesy to each other, obedience to the laws, and submission to the powers that be, are equally urgent to secure the public welfare.

It will be unnecessary to enlarge upon this point, because the evils of insubordination are universally known and lamented. The man who sets at defiance the laws under which he lives and by which he is protected, be his station in life whatever it may, has no regards for the rights and property of his neighbor. What at first was simple fraud becomes dishonesty. A defect in the accredited rulers and governors of any society, induces distrust and disaffection, as insubordination sometimes terminates in rebellion; and the chain of crime leads on by gradual links to every species of disorder; which is the destruction of human happiness. Whatever may have a tendency to prevent such unhappy results must be considered of great public utility. And such is Freemasonry, as will appear from a very slight view of the laws and constitutions of the Order.

These laws and constitutions have been constructed on the principle of *preventing* the commission of crime; thus, rendering *punishment* unnecessary. It is not often that the extreme penalties of the Order are inflicted on Masons, because admonition is generally sufficient to E reduce the desired effect. "If a brother err, admonish him,—perhaps he may be saved," says the most sacred of all books. In like manner the constitutions of Masonry provide, that if a brother shall behave in such a way as to disturb the harmony of the lodge, he shall thrice be formally admonished by the W. M.; and if he persists in his irregular conduct, he will be subject to punishment according to the provisions named in the by-laws of the lodge, except it shall be considered necessary or prudent to report the case to the P. G. Master. But no member can be expelled without due notice being given him of the charge which has been preferred against him, and of the time appointed for its consideration, that he may have a full opportunity of proving his innocence. And in no case can a brother be excluded from his lodge on any charge, except a statement of the cause of his exclusion be forwarded to the Grand and P. G. Masters.

This is in strict conformity with the ancient charge of Masonry, which concludes with these truly excellent directions: "All these charges you are to observe, and also those that shall be communicated to you in another way; cultivating brotherly love, the foundation and cap-stone, the cement and glory, of this ancient fraternity; avoiding all wrangling and quarreling, slandering and backbiting; not permitting others to slander any honest brother, but defending his character and doing him all good offices as far as is consistent with your own honor and safety, but no farther; that all mankind may see the benign influence of Masonry, as all true Masons have done from the beginning of the world, and will do to the end of time."

These appropriate lessons are reduced to practice, and beautifully illustrated in the government of the lodge. Here we find power blended with gentleness, justice with mercy, and strict discipline tempered by harmony and peace. A disposition which produces that concord and agreement amongst the brethren which have characterized the proceedings of Masonry from its first initiation, when the absence of metal tools was intended to symbolize the harmony and union of the members, and have caused it to outlive all other societies of a similar nature which have severally risen, flourished, and decayed, throughout the whole of its quiet and steady progress along the resistless stream of time.

Its operation has realized the picture of a well-regulated and happy society, described by a writer of the last century, where order and harmony are preserved, where peace, tenderness, love, and affection reign, untainted with discord, un-embittered by strife or animosity, because there is a constant and unwearied endeavor to serve and oblige each other. Such a society is doubtless a sight well pleasing in the eyes of that God who formed the members of it. It is an emblem of the whole frame of nature, the glorious fabric of the universe, built by the divine Architect, whose Wisdom ordained it symmetry and proportions; by whose Strength each part is made to be perfect in itself, and to contribute at the tame time to the Beauty, magnificence, and duration of the whole.

Obedience and subordination are virtues which will conduce, in an eminent degree, to the production of this desirable state of order and happiness. And it is an established principle in Masonry, that "such is the nature of our constitution, that as some must of necessity rule and teach, as others must of course learn to submit and obey. *Humility, in both, is an essential duty.*" The most ancient charges provide "that every Master Mason and Fellow that hath trespassed against the Craft shall stand to the correction of other Masters and Fellows to make him accord;" the laws against Master and Fellow being equally stringent. The above virtues, therefore, in both are absolutely requisite to produce the regularity and order which constitute the distinguishing excellence of a lodge of Masons. Society cannot exist without subordination. States and empires fall into ruin and decay, if deprived of the master-hand which presides at the helm to pilot the vessel in safety. The members depend on the correct conduct of the head, as the head depends on the obedience of the members. If law be violated or duty neglected by either party, nothing can be expected to ensue but anarchy and confusion; and this in Masonry would destroy the character of a lodge. Without these ingredients, the cup of bliss would be imperfect; as may be evidenced by the degraded state of those who have set these virtues at defiance. They linger through a miserable life, in continual dread lest the laws they have renounced should rebound with fatal violence, and crush them into ruin. Peace is a stranger to their hearts, and they increase the evil tenfold by endeavoring to drown their apprehensions in the turbid ocean of intoxication. But a habit of obedience produces a meek and quiet spirit, extracts all bitterness from the dream of life, and by a well-regulated system of mutual forbearance and subordination, produces that peace of mind which passeth all understanding.

In the details of the masonic Order, this virtue is carried oat to its utmost perfection; and by habituating the fraternity to an experience of its salutary effects, they are disposed to extend its practice to all the affairs of life; thus affording an example to others all the comfort and happiness which it super induces. Masons are taught to "rule and govern their passions, and to keep a tongue of good report," and while they obey this salutary injunction, they impart a silent lesson to the community amongst which they live, of the serenity of mind which is sure to spring from a strict observance of discipline and social order.

The beautiful arrangement which distinguishes all the proceedings of a lodge of Masons, will be illustrated by the opinion of an experienced Grand Matter (H. R. H. the late Duke of Sussex), who thus instructed the brethren, _ex cathedra_ **(With the full authority of office)**; "It must afford un-initiated individuals matter for deep reflection and consideration, when they see persons of a variety of opinions, of different feelings and religions, entertaining, in fact, all the differences upon politics and religion which are the most capable of exciting the passions, and arraying man against man assembling together in one great cause, and, burying all minor feelings, join cordially in the great work of benefitting society at large by contributing not only their exertions, but their example, in the promoting of everything that is liberal—everything calculated to heighten the character of man. If brethren, when they enter this society, do not reflect upon the principles on which it is founded; if they do not act upon the obligations which they have voluntarily undertaken to discharge, the sooner they retire from the Order, the better it will be for Masonry, and the more creditable for themselves, I am satisfied that the brethren whom I am now addressing do not want any such exhortation. But I think it necessary to impress upon them these facts, because, not only from the high position which I hold, but likewise from the number of years which I have had the honor of belonging to our noble institution, I may be allowed to express my opinion as to the duties which every member of the Craft is bound to perform. When I first determined to become a Freemason, it was a matter of very serious consideration with me; and I can assure the brethren that it was at a period when I had the power of well considering the matter; for it was not in the boyish days of my youth, but at the more mature age of twenty-five or twenty-six years. I did not take it up as a light and trivial matter, but as a grave and serious concern of my life. *I worked my way diligently, passing through all the different offices* of Junior and Senior Warden, Master of a lodge, then Deputy Grand Master, until I finally closed it by the proud station, which I have now the honor to hold. Therefore, having studied it, having reflected upon it, I know the value of the institution; and I may venture to say, that in all my transactions through life, the rules and principles laid down and prescribed by our Order have been, to the best of my faculties, strictly followed. *And if I have been of any use to society at large, it must be attributed, in a great degree, to the impetus derived from Masonry.*"

In a lodge, the strictest government is displayed. Every officer has a place assigned to him. He knows it, and faithfully performs its duties. The Master stands in the east, to instruct by his wisdom; the Senior Warden in the west, to support by his strength; and the Junior Warden in the south, to adorn by his beauty. Even the assistant officers have their specific duties to discharge, and never attempt to exceed them. The brethren listen with attention to the lessons of virtue and morality which emanate from the rising sun, like rays of brilliant light, and learn to profit by obedience and submission to his will and pleasure.

Nothing can be more beautiful than to behold a well-regulated lodge in the exercise of masonic labor. It is a sight which angels would approve of. No disputes or contradictions or opinions can possibly arise, and

> *"The only contention 'mongst' Masons can be,*
> *Who better can work, or who better agree."*

What a French writer says of the delightful plains of Lausanne, will apply to the peace, harmony, and brotherly love, which characterize a Mason's lodge.—"I should wish to end my days in these charming solitudes, far retired from the tumultuous scenes of the world, from avarice and deceit, where a thousand innocent pleasures are enjoyed and renewed without end. There we escape from profligate discourse, from unmeaning prattle, from envy, detraction, and jealousy. Smiling plains, the extent of which the astonished eye is incapable of measuring, and which it is impossible to see without admiring the goodness of the divine Creator; so many different animals wandering peaceably among each other, whose opposite propensities there meet and assimilate; with so many wonders of nature wooing the mind to awful contemplation."

These principles are publicly exhibited in masonic processions, where all is order and decorum. The regulations are so perfect, that everything is precisely where it ought to be. No irregularities are observable, and every individual occupies the station assigned to him according to rank, office, or seniority. It is this which makes a masonic procession such an object of universal interest; and it is totally unattainable by any other order or body of men. The very motion of a body of Masons conveys an idea of peace and tranquility; and, like Balaam, when viewing the camp of Israel, the spectator is entranced, and ready to exclaim—"How goodly are thy tents, O Jacob, and thy tabernacles, O Israel!"

CHAPTER IV

Having in former papers shown what Freemasonry is, I shall conclude this series by a demonstration of what it is not. It is not a system of Rosicrucianism, Iluminism, or Alchemy; nor does it pretend to any exclusive knowledge of the invisible world, or of elemental spirits; and an additional proof that Freemasonry renders essential benefits to society, is the absence of superstition, or a tendency, which we see developed in some of its phases amidst every grade of human life, to interfere with the dispensations of an all wise Providence, by the use of charms, amulets, or the agency of supernatural causes. A modern writer thus explains the origin of amulets: "When men, without disavowing the supreme Lord of all, undertook to relieve him from the care of their own small affairs, which they transferred to inferior agents, they were long thought of attracting and fixing the beneficent attention and influence of those agents, by placing in their houses, or by attaching to their persons, certain symbolical or representative figures, which they appropriated lo their determined use, with such rites and astrological or other observances as they judged suited to the purpose. They are then the symbols, and draw to him the benevolent attention of those powers which are deemed to stand between man and that great and awful Being; whom he thinks he cannot decorously trouble with the relatively small concerns of his family and home. The practical tendency of this to become a low idolatry in the end, we need not indicate."

I have thought it necessary to devote a paper to this subject, because it should seem that in the fifteenth century, the fraternity were somewhat addicted to these forbidden arts, if any dependence may be placed on a MS., said to have been deposited in the Bodleian Library at Oxford, and published in almost every masonic work which appeared during the last century, as a proof that its genuineness was undisputed by the fraternity of that period. In this MS., we find the following question and answer: "*What do the Maconnes concele and hyde? They concele the arte of ffyndynge neue artes, and thatt ys for here owne proffytte and preise. They concelethe the arte of wunder-werckynge, and of foresaynge thynges to comme, that so thay same artes may not be usedde of the wyckedde to an euyell ende. Thay also concelethe the arte of chaunges, the wey of wynnynge the faculties of Abrac, the skylle of becommynge gude and parfyghte wylhouten the holpynges of fete and hope: and the universelle longage of Maconnes.*"

On this passage, Mr. Locke acknowledged himself to be in the dark; and Preston adds—"His being in the dark concerning the meaning of *the faculty of Abrac*, I am not surprised at, nor can conceive how he could otherwise be. Abrac is an abbreviation of the word ABRACA-DABRA. In the days of ignorance and superstition, that word had a magical signification; but the explanation is now lost."

It appears, however, to be generally understood that the word Abrac, Abrasax, or Abracadabra, was derived from the name of Abraham, the father of the faithful, and was given by Basilides to Mithras, or the sun, as the representative of the supreme deity, or the SUN OF RIGHTEOUSNESS. Basilides was a Pythagorean of Alexandria, and when he embraced Christianity, he introduced the dogmata of that philosopher into his system; which constituted a medley, that is thus described in a letter of the Emperor Hadrian to Servianus, the consul, in which he says—"I have learned, my dear Servianus, that Egypt is an inconstant and fluctuating nation, which is always ready to revolt on the least excitement. The Christians are worshippers of Serapis; and some of the votaries of that deity have been elevated to the dignity of bishops. There is, however, in reality no religion amongst them, neither Jewish nor Samaritan, heathen or Christian. When the patriarch goes into Egypt, one party will call upon him to worship Serapis, and another Jesus Christ, in short, it is a most seditious, vain, and insolent nation."

To carry out the Pythagorean principles, Basilides enjoined on his disciples a nominal silence of five years, in imitation of the quinquennial silence of the Pythagoreans. The word Abrasax, or Abraxas, being composed of seven letters, referred equally to the seven heavens, and the same number of subordinate angels or intelligences, as their governors; for the Basilideans considered the seven planets to be the entire universe, and consequently, God. And as the annual course of the sun was accomplished in 365 days, they conjured up the names of that number of spirits, and distributed the days amongst them. According to this belief, the primogenial mind proceeded from Abraxas, which produced the Logos or Word; from whence came Phronoesis or Prudence, Sophia and Dynamis, or wisdom and strength, principalities, powers, and angels; and from these, other angels to the number of 365, who were supposed to have the government of so many celestial orbs committed to their care. And it so happens that the numerical powers of the letters in this cabaliatical word, in Greek, make together the exact number of 365, thus;

$$A \quad B \quad P \quad A \quad X \quad A \quad E$$
$$1 + 2 + 100 + 1 + 60 + 1 + 200 = 365$$

St. Austin charges Basilides with maintaining the heresy of three hundred and sixty-five heavens, which were the creators of the world. This seems to be a mistake; for he ascribed that work to the ministry of the seven angels who preside over the heavens, and called the supreme power DEMIURGUS, or IAΩ, who is the same as Jehovah of the Jews. Archbishop Tenison terms the religion of the pseudo-Christians, who embraced the doctrine of the Gnostics, "a sort astrological magic;" and adds, "every heretic feigneth what pleaseth himself, and then he worshippeth his own fiction. Thus did Marcion with his idle deity, Valentius with his thirty Eons, and

Basilides with his god! Abraxas."

This great Basilidean deity is affirmed in the MS., above quoted, to have been introduced into the Freemasonry of the middle ages by the operative Masons, whose works still excite our admiration and delight. It appears to have been used as an amulet or talisman, and its virtues were supposed to be concentrated in a gem or crystal, with sundry figures engraved on each face, amongst which the sacred names of the deity occupied conspicuous situations. This being ritually consecrated by certain prescribed observances, was delivered to the individual in those favor it had been constructed, and worn about the person with implicit faith in its efficacy to restore health, to avert danger, to inspire love or hatred, to protect hidden treasures, or as a safeguard against fire, the sword, or any other accident that threatens life: and the eastern nations believed that by friction, as was the case with the lamp of Aladdin, the presence of a spirit would he evoked.

Montfaucon has furnished engravings of some hundreds of these gems or amulets, and divides them into seven classes, *viz.* — 1. The abraxas, with the head of a cock and legs of serpents. 2. In the form of a lion, or some of its component parts, united with the bodies of serpents. 3. With the figure or name of Serapis. 4. Of the anubis and the scarabaeus. 6. With the figure of Apollo or the sun, in human shape, sometimes furnished with wings. 6. With inscriptions, generally referring to the Redeemer of mankind. 7. With names of the powers referred to in the Basilidean system.

To show in its true light, the puerile superstition which was displayed in the dark ages by the use of these amulets, respecting which even the philosophic Burton could say—"Amulets and things to be borne about I find prescribed, taxed by some, approved by others; and I say with Renodeus, they are not altogether to be rejected;" and to demonstrate the implicit faith which was placed in their reputed efficacy, it may not be uninteresting to subjoin a few remarks on this abstruse subject, founded on the classification of the above indefatigable antiquary.

1. The first class of gems is furnished with the head of a cock, having a human body, with two serpents in the place of legs, the head of each serpent serving as a foot. This figure is sometimes portrayed brandishing other things, the name of IAO, a remarkable Greek inscription to this effect: — "Give me grace and victory, because I have pronounced thy INEFFABLE NAME." Another has the same figure with Fortune standing on the cock's head, and inscribed underneath, IAO; while on the reverse we find I A O-A B R A C A S. On some we find the names of the Basilidean angels, Michael, Gabriel, Uriel, Raphael, Amanael, Prosoraiel, Yabsoe, &c.; on others Mithras, Abrasax, Sabaoth, &c. In the ancient mythology, the cock was a symbol of the sun, because he foretells its rising; and amongst the pseudo Christians who invented and used these amulets, Jesus Christ was identified with the sun, and therefore aptly represented by a man with a cock's head; and their possessors were reputed to be under his especial protection as Lord of the year, depicted, as we have just seen, by Abraxas, and also by the word Mithras, or rather MEITHRIS, which equally, according to the Greek notation, express 365, and by the annual course of the earth round the sun.

2. In the second class, we find Abraxas in the form of a lion, to symbolize the lion of the tribe of Judah; and some of them △ contain the word IOY AC on the reverse, and a man with a lion's head, holding in his left hand the head of the traitor Judas, and an inscription implying, "*the lion of the tribe of Judah has overcome!*" Many of these are inscribed with the words Mithras, IAO, Abraxas, Anubis, &c. On one we find Harpocrates, the god of science, seated on a tree springing from the back of a lion, with a whip in his hand, and a finger on his mouth; and another seems to indicate that the amulets of this class were intended as sanitary nostrums, for it has a Greek inscription implying, "*Preserve in health the stomach of Proclus.*" Some of them have the head of the lion radiated, and a serpent's body, with the word X Ns O U B I C on the reverse. Sometimes, instead of the initial X there is substituted a ✛, which Salmasius interprets as one of the thirty-six deans which, according

to the Gnostics, presided over the zodiac. Montfaucon, however, rejects this interpretation, and thinks the - ✛ - represents the first letter in the alphabet, which will make ANUBIS, an Egyptian deity, whose name very frequently occurs on these gems.

3. We come now to those that have either the inscription or figure of Serapis; and these are fully illustrated on plate 50 of the second volume of Montfaucon'a great work. On one of these Isis is represented upon the flower of the lotus, and before her is an ape, or the corcopithecus,

with the inscription, "ONE JUPITER SERAPIS". On the reverse is the name Abraxas, and the words, "*Give grace to Alexander,*" which shows it to have been an amulet of good luck. On another, Serapis is represented as holding a figure of Victory in his hand, with an inscription in cabalistic characters. Serapis has at her feet the three-headed dog Cerberus, which appears to intimate that he was sometimes identified with Pluto. Another has the head of Serapis surmounted by a calathus, with an inscription in Greek, "*Preserve me*;" which proves beyond a doubt that these gems were intended as amulets of protection.

4. The fourth class is not confined to the figure of Anubis, although that Egyptian divinity predominates. Here we find the sacred name I A O of frequent recurrence; and in some of them, Anubis holds in one hand a palm branch, in allusion to the Savior's triumphal entry into Jerusalem; for the early Christians used to carry palm branches in processions five days before the anniversary; of the crucifixion, which they placed on the altar, on the other hand Anubis carries a crown, as a symbol of the crown of glory promised to those who endure faithfully to the end. Many gems of this class bear the scarabseus, or sacred beetle of Egypt; and they are usually perforated, for the convenience of being suspended from the neck by a ligature, as amulets of protection from danger. The beetle was an emblem of the sun. Amongst other animals, the serpent, which had a similar reference, was a favorite symbol with the Basilideans; and we accordingly find it impressed on a specimen of the Abraxas.

We have also on another gem and cross, which perhaps Withers had in view when he often quoted passage:

> *A serpent raised above the letter tau*
> *Aspiring to the crowne, is figured here;*
> *From whence a Christian moral we may draw,*
> *Which worth our good regarding will appear.*
> *The crosse doth show that suffering is the way;*
> *The serpent seems to teach me, that if I*
> *Will overcome, I must then not assay*
> *To force it; but myself thereto applye;*
> *For by embracing what we shall not shunne,*
> *We wind about the crosse, til we arise*
> *Above the same; and then what prise is wonne*
> *The crowne that over tops it, signifies.*

Endless serpents enclosing mystical characters are common; and there is one with a curious inscription, importing that *though the serpent roar like a lion, it is as meek as a lamb*. Montfaucon has given, amongst numerous others, a specimen of a very extraordinary gem, marked 18 on plate 50, which has upon one side two serpents twisted round stakes fixed in the ground, with an altar, a cup, and two stars in the canter. The other side is full of symbols of birds, serpents, men on foot and on horseback, two human busts, one radiated, and the other with a crescent; the explanation of which that great antiquary professes himself unable to penetrate. The Gnostics venerated the serpent, which they esteemed to be Christ, and therefore the serpent and stake might be intended to represent the brazen serpent of Moses. Tertullian informs us, that they preferred the serpent to Jesus Christ, because it was endued with the knowledge of good and evil; and therefore, it was that Moses selected it as his symbol of health. And this doctrine appears to be confirmed by another gem, which has on one side IAOSA-BAO, and on the other M O S U S.

5. The human forms displayed in the class of Abraxas, are sometimes without wings, at others they are furnished with two, like those of an angel; with four, like the cherubic figure of Ezekiel; and in some cases with six, in imitation, doubtless, of the seraphim of Isaiah. The human figure is understood to represent the sun, as a symbol of Christ, who, by the Theosophists of the last century, was considered as the spiritual philosopher's stone; and the reverse of some of these amulets presents the word CHEROUBI, for angels and cherubim formed a part of the Basilidean system. Montfaucon, however, thinks that "these Abraxas having always relation to the sun, the wing were designed to show the swiftness of his course." Like the former, we frequently find on this class the words IAO, ADONAT, and SABAOTB. One contains an Egyptian mummy, with the Greek words for preserve me, and, on the reverse, Sabao, Several of them contain figures of the deities of Greece and Rome; as Jupiter, Apollo, Hercules, Canopus, Diana, with her bow and arrows, inscribed with the name of the angel GABRIEL, the three graces, &c. One an inscribed, "*There is but one Jupiter Serapis.*" Thus, uniting in a single individual, the Greek and Egyptian deity. Another presents a figure of Fortune, with an inscription promising "*good fortune to Xistus.*" Several are impressed with cabalistic characters, which none understand but the fabricators, and perhaps they themselves were ignorant of their true interpretation. The figure of Canopus, however, was doubtless a talisman of health, for it bore on the reverse the pentalpha, or endless triangle, which constituted the far-famed seal of Solomon, and was used by these fanatics for the purpose of driving away diseases, as the people of the east applied it to the prevention or cure of witchcraft.

6. The Abraxas of these clans are constructed of a much larger size for the purpose of containing extended inscriptions; and few of them have any figures or symbolical representations. These inscriptions consist generally of a series of cabalistic words, intermingled with the names of the Basilidean Intelligences, and are intended as a preservative against the power of evil demons. The

words IAO and SABAOTH are abundantly used, as well as those of ABRACAS, SALLAMAXA, BAMAIACHA, AGANACHBA, SAMMAZ, AZALLIAB, and many others, which are the names of the above powers. Some are intended for the protection of cities, others to guard individuals from disease, coproduce fecundity, and for a happy deliverance from child-bearing. Montfaucon was in possession of a cast sent from Italy, of a talisman of this class, which had on one side the head of Alexander the Great covered with a lion's skin, and on the reverse an ass suckling a colt, with the inscription D. N. I H V X P S DEI FILIVS. He also describes a crystal which was celebrated for consoling spirits. It is globular, oval, and transparent, with the name of various Basilidean powers visible within it. It is an extraordinary specimen, but the explanation is too long for the introduction here.

7. We now come to the seventh and last class of these gems, which contain the names of the celestial powers or Eons of the Gnostics. They were 365 in number, each having a separate portion of the human body assigned to its protection. Many of these names are lost, but Montfaucon has preserved upwards of a hundred, most of them being barbarous, and some unpronounceable. These amulets generally contain figures of the constellations, planets, and celestial signs, and some bear all the signs of the zodiac. On an amulet with five faces, there are so many inscriptions, each commencing with a different version of the Sacred Name, thus: JEOHOVA, JEOVAHO, JAVOIEO, EOVIAOE, and EIEDIOA. It appears to have been a kind of palladium or amulet for the protection of a city; as the meaning of the inscription is: *"Jehovah, Holy One, Preserve the city of the Mileshians and its inhabitants from all dangers."*

I conclude this extended dissertation with an explanation, out of the same author, of "the facultie of Abrac, or Abracadabra", which was used by the Basilideans in the cure of agues and other diseases; and the directions for its efficacious application were as follows. It was to be written several times on a piece of paper, in

INFLUENCE ON THE MORAL AND SOCIAL CONDITION OF MAN

eleven lines, retrenching one letter in each line, until it terminated in an inverted cone. The paper was then to be folded and sealed according to art, and tied around the neck of the patient. The cure, it is said, was certain to follow.

Quintus Serenus Sominicus, a Basilidean physician, left among his papers the following verses:

Inscribes charte quod dictur ABRACAAABRA Saepis, et subter repetis, ted detrahe summam Et magis atque magis desint elementa figuris Singula, qus Mraper rapies, et caetera figes, Donec in angustam redigatur litera cunum; His lino nexis collum redimire memento.

```
ABRACADABRA
ABRACADABR
ABRACADAB
ABRACADA
ABRACAD
ABRACA
ABRAC
ABRA
ABR
AB
A
```

Such were the absurd superstitions which have been charged on the Freemasons of the Medieval ages; but they were consonant with universal belief, and do not apply to the Freemasons alone. And if Freemasonry in those early times did countenance these superstitious practices, it was because they constituted a moral epidemic which prevailed through every grade of society. But the entire fabric of superstition has been swept away from the system of Masonry as it is now practiced. The floor of our lodges is cleaned from the pollution by a three-fold consecration which converts it into holy ground; and we indignantly repel the insinuation that such fancies are there inculcated as branches of a cabaliatical science.

Some kind of superstition has always distinguished particular ages. As witness, the reputed miraculous powers of the early Ascetics, and the custom which St. Austin complains of, that some of Satan's instruments, who professed the exercise of these arts, mixed up the name of Christ with their enchantments lo seduce Christians to receive the doctrine as a sweet potion, which might conceal the heresy, and make men drink it to their destruction. And also in our own country, from the royal touch of Edward the Confessor, through all the absurdities of demoniacal agency, alchemy, the cramp-rings of Wolsey and his royal patron, witchcraft, necromancy, charms, spells, &c., which were not confined to the ignorant, but were practiced by kings, princes, priests, and philosophers, down to the delusions of Cagliostro, Mesmer, St. Germain, and their compeers of the last century, and the reveries of Johanna Southcote and Carlile, with the quack nostrums and galvanic rings of our own times.

The bare suspicion of the fraternity being addicted to these Rosicrucian mummeries, pointed the pen of Barriel with gall when he roundly stated, "The principal objection against me is, that I have confounded Freemasonry with the ancient Rosicrucians. My answer is, that if all Masons are not Rosicrucians, all Rosicrucians are Masons; and the first three degrees are, and always have been, a novitiate for Rosicrucianism; and I should be glad to see it proved that those occult mysteries do not belong to the three first degrees. I think I can prove that they do." This reasoning is entirely fallacious. Barruel asserts that he is able to identify these follies with the three first degrees of Masonry. Why has he not done so, when the proof would have been so important a confirmation of his argument? The reason is clear,—he was unable to do it. For it is well known to all the fraternity, and to our opponents also, if they possessed sufficient candor to acknowledge it, that Freemasonry has been completely purged from all such charlatanarie, if ever it formed a part of the system, which is extremely doubtful, and is presented to the public as a pure and rational institution, which unites science and morals with benevolence and charity, and recommended the practice of virtue to promote human happiness in this world, in the hope, if properly regulated, it will lead, in the next, to a house not made with hands, eternal in die heavens.

(The word "Abracadabra" was used to fight against diseases during the 450 BC, when the Romans suffered from a plague of malaria, which was assigned a very important role in the decline of the great Roman Empire. The Romans never imagined that the mosquito was the transmitter of the disease.

For them, malaria came from a magic source and as such, it must be combated in the same way. One of the ways to combat this disease is found in the medical text of the 3rd century, Quintus Serenus Sammonicus, in which the word "Abracadabra" is mentioned for the first time:

Then the piece of paper should be rolled up and wrapped in cloth, worn hanging from the neck as if it were a talisman, for a period of nine days, then the talisman should be thrown into a river whose current was to the east.

On the other hand, some experts find it in the Hebrew expressions, "Ab, rauch, dabar" (father, holy spirit, word) or "Abrai silk brai" (out of evil spirit).)

THE EMBLEMATICAL REFERENCES OF THE SUN IN A MASONIC LODGE

In some of our ancient Tracing boards, we find the letter G inscribed within a Blazing Star or Sun, which has induced the opinion that Freemasonry is but a continuation of the solar superstition, as it was practiced in the mysteries of heathen nations. Thus, a writer of our own country says; "Masonry is the remains of the religion of the ancient Druids, who, like the magi of Persia, and the priests of Heliopolis in Egypt, were priests of the Sun. They paid worship to this luminary as the visible agent of a great invisible first cause, whom they styled *Time without limits*. In Masonry, many of the ceremonies of the Druids are preserved in their original state, at least without any parody. With them, the Sun is the great emblematical ornament of Masonic Lodges and Masonic dresses; it is the central figure on their aprons, and they wear it also pendant on the breast in their Lodges and in their processions. It has the face of a man. As the study and contemplation of the Creator in the works of the creation, of which the Sun, as the great visible agent of that Being, was the object of the Druids adoration, all their religious rites and ceremonies had reference to the apparent progress of the Sun through the twelve signs of the zodiac, and his influence upon the earth. The Masons adopt the same practices. The roof of their Temples or Lodges," he continues, "is ornamented with a sun, and the floor is a representation of the variegated face of the earth, either by carpeting or Mosaic work." And therefore, he concludes that Freemasonry, like the religion of the Druids, is a system of sun worship.

It is true, these are the words of a professed atheist, but they have been adopted in substance by many a serious Christian, to throw discredit upon Masonry; and used as a powerful and unanswerable argument to identify it with the heathen mysteries. An hypothesis which, if true, would place the Indian Vedas, the Persian Shaster, the Koran of Mahomet, the Jewish Mikra, and the Christian Gospel, on one and the same level. There can be little doubt, but the spurious Freemasonry recommended and practiced the solar superstition a devotion which was not confined to any one country or people, but was as widely disseminated as the migrations from the plain of Shinar. When a new Lodge, or place of initiation was to be established, the hierophant sought out some natural cavern, and in default of this he excavated a rock artificially, and formed it into a series of galleries and apartments which would be convenient for the exercise of the secret rites. These usually terminated in a sacellum, which was furnished and decorated for effect. The fitting up of this room or saloon formed a matter of grave consideration; but, however the enrichments might be as versified in other respects, it always contained a series of astronomical emblems, which were closely connected with the mythology of the country, and consisted generally of a zodiac and central Sun, with planets and stars revolving about it; for they compared the Deity, amidst his host of mediators, to the Sun in his career through the heavenly bodies; and in the euresis of the initiation, or revivification and raising of the patron demon, who was no other than the Sun, it was symbolized by a new-born infant, seated on the calyx of the lotus, or water lily. The candidate was considered the representative of that holy personage, in his character of the great benefactor of the universe.

The most ancient astronomers were so struck with the dimensions of the solar orb, and its properties of light and heat, that, under the influence of reason only, they pronounced it to be the seat of the ever-living God. As it appeared to be the fountain of life, and source of all their pleasures, they assigned it as the residence of the Supreme Being, and the inferior deities were placed in the planets and fixed stars. According to Macrobius, *"quod Sol auctor spiritus caloris ac luminis humanse vitse genitor et custos est; et ideo nascentis daemon; id est, Deus creditur.*" Hence, the Sun became the chief object of worship, in all nations where the spurious Freemasonry was practiced. Tacitus says, "*proprius honor Soli, cui est vetus aedes apud circum.*" Pertullian describes the mode of adoration. "*Plerique affectione adorandi, aliquando etiam celestia, ad Solis initium labra vibratis.*"

There appears to have been a universal disposition, in the structure of the spurious Freemasonry, to assimilate the principal deity with the Sun; whose figure, as an immense blazing star, always occupied a prominent situation in their caverns of initiation. Macrobius asks, Saturnus "*ipse, qui auctor est temporum, et ideo a Grsecis immutata litera quasi, vocatur, quid aliud nisi Sol inteUigendus est?*" And he occupies seven chapters of the first book of his Saturnalia in proving that Saturn, Jupiter, Pan, Nemesis, Osiris and Orus, Adonis and Isis, Atys and Serapis, Salus, Hercules, Mercury, Esculapius, Mars, and Apollo, were all of them the Sun. Plato denominates Jupiter the Sun; Mars, according to Faber, was Mars, the Great Sun; Mercury, on the same authority, was M'Erech—Ur, the great burning divinity of the ark; Bacchus is celebrated by Sophocles as the leader of the host of heaven; Apollo is well known as the Sun, and is called Sol, as Cicero informs us, "*vel quia solus ex omnibus sideribus tantus est; vei quia cum axortus est; obscuratibus omnibus, Solis apparet*" Mithras was denominated by Zoroaster, and referred to the same luminary.

In like manner, the Hindoo deity was the Sun, under his three well-known forms: Brahma rising in the east; Vishnu southing at his meridian, and Siva, setting in the west. The aborigines of America worshipped the Sun under the name of the Great Father; and the Peruvians celebrated a grand festival in his honor, at the autumnal equinox; a period when their divinity in advancing from the north passes over the equator, and may be seen to repose himself upon the pillars of his temples. In the Gothic system of spurious Freemasonry, practiced by the northern nations of Europe, the same reference is obvious. Their god Thor was the Sun, and he was depicted with twelve stars in a circle round his head, to represent the twelve signs of the zodiac. In the description of heaven in the Edda, universal space is denominated "a hall," wherein are twelve seats for the gods, besides the throne of the universal father or the Sun.

The Celtic mysteries which were practiced in our own island, were constructed on the same general principles; being instituted in honor of Hu, the solar divinity; who is represented by the Bardic writers as the ethereal being who is belted with the rainbow; and in Egypt, the girdle of the hierophant, which was frequently a serpent, to express his eternity, was emblematical of the Sun's orbit The grand periods of initiation and festival in Britain were regulated by the times when the solar deity attained the equinoctial and solstitial points, and then the Bealtine fires were kindled, and hymns were chaunted, and hands were kissed in honor of the Sun, which was esteemed, in the degeneracy of the Druidical mysteries, the one governor of the world.

Now this is legitimate Sun worship, as it was undoubtedly practiced in the spurious Freemasonry; and the emblems were always present in the sacellum of the Lodge, or cavern of initiation; and nothing can show the purity of our own system of Freemasonry in a clearer and more amiable light than its unequivocal condemnation of such practices. Instead of indulging the pollutions of the solar worship, Freemasonry, as we practice it, recommends and enforces an adoration of that Great Being whose laws the Sun, the moon, and stars obey. It is true; we use many of the same emblems as the spurious system, but they are regarded merely as references to human virtues, and not to a personation of the divinity. "When the Free and accepted Mason," say our lectures, "exalts his view to the more noble and elevated parts of nature, and surveys the celestial orbs, how great is his astonishment. If, on the principles of true philosophy, he contemplates the Sun, the moon, the stars, and the whole concave of heaven, his pride is humbled, and he is lost in awful admiration. The immense magnitude of those bodies, the regularity and rapidity of their motions, and the vast extent of space through which they move, are equally inconceivable; and, as far as they exceed human comprehension, baffle his most daring ambition, till, lost in the immensity of the theme, he sinks into his primitive insignificance. By geometry, we trace nature through her various windings, to her most concealed recesses. By it we discover the power, the wisdom, and the goodness of the Great Architect of the universe, and view with delight the proportions which connect this vast machine. By it we discover, how the planets move in their different orbits, and demonstrate their various revolutions. By it we account for the return of seasons, and the variety of scenes which each season displays to the discerning eye. Numberless worlds are around us; all framed by the same Divine Artist, which roll through the vast expanse, and are all conducted by the same unerring law."

But while Freemasonry thus makes use of its symbols to inculcate great moral truths, it never falls into the extravagancies which disfigured its spurious imitator. For it is remarkable, that while we are considering the solar deity of the mysteries as a male person, and the resolution of all the hero gods into that one luminary, we are struck with a very extraordinary anomaly when we refer to the female deities of the gentile world, who are often described as being of the male sex. Thus, Venus was a personification of the moon. By some she was called Juno; by others, Isis, Vesper, and Lucifer; but she was sometimes represented with a beard, &c. as a man. Est etiam, says Servius, in his commentary on the Æneid in Cypro *simulacrum barbate Veneris corpore et veste muliebn, cum sceptro et natura virili, quod vocant.* Minerva is thus addressed in the hymns called Orphic. In like manner, the Gothic female deity, Friga or Frea, was of both sexes; sometimes she was worshipped as a female, and at others as a god, depicted in male attire, and armed with a bow and arrows. The moon is spoken of as a male in the Orphic fragments, and was so worshipped at Cabira, among the Albani; and in Greece she was occasionally adored in conjunction with Esculapius. At Antiochea, in Hsidia, atid various other places, temples were dedicated to the rites of Meen Arkaeus, or deus Lunus. So likewise in India, the moon was considered a male deity called Chandra; represented as seated in a chariot drawn by antelopes, with a lunette at his head and another at his feet. The explanation of the fable, I believe is, that when the moon was in conjunction with the Sun it was female, and when in opposition, male.

And equally extraordinary are the absurd fables of the Spurious Freemasonry, which represent Jupiter at one time as the *father* of men; at another, as the mother of the gods; and sometimes as an hermaphrodite. *Jupiter omnipotens Regum Rex ipse Deumque Progenitor, Genetrixque deutn. Deus unus et idem.* - Val Soran ap. Aug. de civ. dei, 1. 4.

On this curious subject, the learned Cudworth thus expresses himself. "Proclus, in the Timaeus says, Jove is both a man and an immortal maid." But this is nothing but a poetic description of, male and female together; they are signifying thereby emphatically the divine fecundity, or the generative and creative power of the deity; was able from himself alone to produce all things. Hene Damascius, the philosopher, writing of the Orphic theology expounds it thus, "The Orphic theology calls the first principle hermaphrodite, or male and female together, thereby denoting that essence which is generative or productive of all things." After all, it is highly probable that this androgynal doctrine might be derived from a passage in the Book of Genesis, which records that man was created male and female, and that God called their name Adam. Some of the Rabbins understand this literally, and assert that the man and woman were created in one person and that God subsequently separated them from each other. Plutarch considered the eternal God as an Intelligence; both male and female—light and life, and that he brought forth another Intelligence, who was the Creator of all things.

My limits will not allow me to go further in detail on this part of the subject; and therefore I must take it for granted that I have adduced sufficient evidence to prove that the Sun was actually worshipped as a god in all the religious mysteries of ancient nations, however the peculiar ceremonies might vary; and that such an impure system of devotion led to the most grievous errors both in faith and practice.

I proceed to contrast this complete identification of the Supreme Deity and Creator of the world with the Sun in the spurious Freemasonry of ancient times, with the references to the same luminary in our own pure and holy system.

The Sun, in our Lodges, is represented merely as a creature in the hand of God to convey benefits to man. Besides, if Freemasonry in the nineteenth century consider the Sun as an object of worship, it may with great propriety be asked, which Sun? for the center of our system forms only a unit amidst the 75,000 systems, each having a central Sun, with which modern discovery has furnished universal space. Freemasonry speaks of the Sun as a fixed body, producing the phenomenon of being always at its meridian height to some part of the earth's surface, from the file revolution of the latter body on its own axis; it speaks of the glorious Sun beheld by the candidate at his first entrance into the Lodge, emerging from darkness in the East, and diffusing light and nourishment to all sublunary things; and represented by the Master, who is placed in the East to open his Lodge as the Sun opens the day, to diffuse light, knowledge, and instruction to the Brethren; to enlighten with true wisdom his Masonic companions, and to guide all his fellow-craftsmen to work out their salvation with fear and trembling. It speaks of the Sun as seen in its meridian splendor, when its vertical rays are most powerful, and the cool south most pleasant, represented by the Junior Warden, who, at the hour of high twelve invites the Brethren to rest from their labors, to repose in the cooling shade, and to regale; and provides for their return to labor in due time, that profit and pleasure may be the mutual result. Freemasonry further regards the Sun setting in the West, and lulling, as it were, all nature to repose, in the person of Senior Warden, who stands in that quarter to close the Lodge by the Master's command, to confer on every Brother the due reward of his merit, to see that none go away dissatisfied, or unimproved in moral virtue and pious resolutions.

Here then we have an evidence, taken from our own peculiar disquisitions of the use we make of the Sun, as a Masonic symbol. It calls our attention to holy things. It is esteemed as an agent—a most stupendous one; I admit—of the power and goodness of God. How can we, as Free and Accepted Masons, after the lessons we hear in the Lodge, look up to the heavens, and behold the sublime order and the vast dimensions of those glorious orbs of light which glitter in the firmament of heaven, with the regularity in which they perform their various revolutions, without humbly and devoutly confessing them to declare the glory of God? How can we meditate on the vast and boundless space in which they move, without acknowledging his handy-work is there? They convey a noble idea of Him whom the Sun, the moon, and the stars obey; and elevate our thoughts and aspirations far beyond all created matter, to the Throne of the Great Creator; that ever present Deity whose All-seeing Eye beholds our actions in the dark as well as in the light—in the absence of the Sun as well as in its presence—in the depths of the most obscure cavern in mountains in the blaze of day—and alike at the bottom of the fathomless ocean at midnight, and under the beams of the meridian Sun. This is the Holy Being whom Masons adore; who "by his excellent wisdom made the heavens; who laid out the earth above the waters; who made great lights; the Sun to rule the day, the Moon and the Stars to govern the night; whose voice shaketh the wilderness, and divideth the flames of fire; whose kingdom is an everlasting kingdom, and his dominion endureth throughout all ages."

The truth of these observations may be proved from our own lectures. In a lucid illustration of the three great pillars of Masonry which form the allegorical support of the Lodge, we find the following exquisite passage. "The universe is the temple of the Deity whom we serve; wisdom, strength, and beauty are about his throne, as pillars of his work, for his wisdom is infinite, his strength is omnipotence, and his beauty shines forth in all his works in symmetry and order. He hath crowned the heavens with stars as with a diadem; *the earth he hath planted as his footstool; the Sun and Moon are messengers of his will, and all his law is concord."*

What can more plainly express the fact that Masons regard the Sun and Moon as messengers of His Almighty will and pleasure, and invest them with no higher rank? Nay, so far is the science of Freemasonry from assigning any undue influence to the Sun, that some of our Brethren of the last century conjectured that it was created for other imposes than to be the glory of the world, by conveying light and nourishment to all things here below. They ventured to suggest the probability that, when all the purposes of its first commission shall have terminated by the destruction of this globe which we inhabit, it will be destined to another office which is equally registered in the designs of Omnipotence, viz., to be the local place of punishment for those unhappy beings on whom the final sentence of reprobation shall be pronounced.

To maintain this opinion, they assumed as an axiom, that the Sun is a body of real, corporeal fire. If anyone, they said, doubt this, let him subject his naked body to its scorching beams; or endure the power of his rays when collected and transmitted through a convex lens. At its present distance from the earth, it is a blessing and a comfort, but a nearer approach would scorch and burn up this globe and all that it contains. This is confirmed by the Sun's magnitude. Tychoi Brahe estimates it to be 139 times larger than the earth; Landsberg says it is 484 times as large, and Flamstead 11,000 times, "I do not think then," concludes Mr. Swinden, "that anyone can have much to object against this hypothesis, either from the nature of the body of the sun, or from the magnitude of it For since it is expressly revealed in the Word of God, that there is such a thing or place as hell-fire; and that the same is appointed for the punishment of an innumerable company of devils and wicked men. And since this is so far from being found a thing impossible, that we have plain demonstrative proof of such a place of fire in the world, abundantly large, and capable of receiving vast, infinite numbers both of devils, and also of the bodies of men; have we not some reason to infer that this is possibly the hell? I am sure no one, without an express revelation from God, can say it is not."

However this may be, the above remarks are sufficient to prove every hypothesis erroneous which tends to charge the Freemasons, or any other body of men who have been blessed with the light of revelation, with an addiction to the solar worship for who in his sober senses would pay divine honors to a place of punishment, or to any creature which God has provided for the benefit of man?

The places of the three superior officers of the Lodge are regulated by the Sun in his three most prominent positions; and the Sun, the Moon, and the Master, form a triad of antitypes, which exhibit these luminaries as agents of the divine Being to work out His beneficent designs, and place one of the Masters duties in a striking and unequivocal point of view. As it is by the benign influence of the two formers if we, as men, are enabled to perform the duties of social life; so, it is by the ceaseless activity and intelligence of the Master, that we, as Masons are enabled to understand and discharge those duties which the Craft requires of us.

Similar references are found throughout all the lectures of symbolical Masonry, the particular instances of which will occur to every well instructed Brother; and they all treat the Sun as a creature—though a very useful one, and a symbol of moral and divine truths—without exhibiting the lightest tendency to create an interest beyond what arises out of its allegorical references. Even the foreign degree of Chevalier du Soleil, or Knight of the Sun, although it leans to deism, and is consequently unworthy to be practiced by a Christian Mason, affords no evidence of an approach to the solar superstition; as will appear from a very brief analysis of the degree, which is seldom practiced in this country, and has only a very equivocal connection with Freemasonry, although it forms a part of the French system of the rite ancient *et accepte*.

THE EMBLEMATICAL REFERENCES OF THE SUN IN A MASONIC LODGE

In this degree the presiding officer is seated in the East where the Sun rises, robed in the colors of the sky at dawn of day, and round his neck a chain of gold, which, as a metal, corresponds with the planet Sol, and both are expressed by a point within a circle, which was anciently considered a symbol of perfection. From this chain, a figure of the meridian Sun in the same metal is suspended; while in his right hand is a scepter terminating in a globe to represent the earth, which is nurtured and made prolific by the Sun's rays. The Warden has also a Sun attached to his collar. These, as we shall soon see, are emblems, but not intended as objects of adoration. When the Lodge or Council is at work, the Sun is said to be at its meridian, while to the profane it is considered low twelve or midnight. It is opened with a public profession of the divine unity, I pass over the ceremonies for obvious reasons, with a simple declaration that they do not bear upon the question, and proceed to the lectures.

These contain explanations of the emblems of the three degrees of symbolical Masonry; the greater and lesser lights, the Tracing-boards, &c., in the following manner. The candidate is addressed by the Grand Master—"Brother, you are already acquainted with the symbol of a Bible, Square, and Compasses; but of its allegorical meaning you remain in ignorance. Be it my duty to enlighten you. The Bible refers to the religion which the first man practiced — the religion of nature. The Compasses teach that God is the central point, as well as the circumference of the universe; and always present to us all. The Square is intended to show that God has made everything equal; while the cubical stone shows that you ought to govern your actions so correctly, as to make them all equal in respect to the sovereign good. The pillars teach you firmness, the tressle-board, the employment of reason, &c."

I do not acquit the professors of this degree of heterodoxy with respect to religious faith, because the symbols are strained to a meaning which their natural signification will not justify; and it would puzzle a plain man to understand how the volume of revelation can be an appropriate symbol of natural religion. Still, I am convinced they are not addicted to the solar worship. Thus, in the Philosophical Lecture, while explaining the reference of the Compasses, they say—"the difference between good and evil in the estimation of God, may be explained by the compasses. While inscribing a circle, the moveable leg of that instrument recedes from the point where it commenced till it arrives at the greatest possible distance; it then approaches nearer and nearer till the line unites, which forms a perfect circumference. This process represents the distance between the several degrees of good and evil; and the completion of the circle is God; whose center is everywhere, and whose circumference is nowhere."

The doctrine throughout corresponds with these specimens. The Sun is said symbolically to represent the divinity of the Supreme Being who created the world; for as there is but one Sun to enlighten and invigorate the earth, so there is but one God whom we ought to worship. The physical lecture adds, the Sun points out the infinity of God's will, as the only source of light and benefit to his creatures.

That the reader may understand the references in this degree more perfectly, I subjoin its Tracing-board. The explanation of its emblems would not accord with my limits. I shall confine myself to the two most obvious. The triangle in a circle with the Sun in the center is a symbol of the eternity of God, who, like the perfect circle, has neither beginning nor end. And the four conjoined triangles point out the four principal duties of a Mason, fraternal love; conferring benefits; believing nothing till it be clearly demonstrated; and doing to others as you would have them do to you. From all this, it will appear evident that even the Knights of the Sun were not solar devotees. And it will be amply sufficient to show the real value which Masons in general place on this significant emblem.

THE EMBLEMATICAL REFERENCES OF THE SUN IN A MASONIC LODGE

ON THE OBJECTIONS OF SOME OF THE ANGLO-INDIAN CLERGY

There is nothing perfect under the sun. The Almighty disposer of events has ordered it for wise and beneficent purposes, secret to us, that the attainment of knowledge should be progressive. Thus, the endowments or qualities of inanimate stones are exceeded by those which appear inherent in plants; their properties must succumb to the instinct of animals, and that to the reason of man. But man, compared with the higher range of beings, is as imperfect as the rough stone compared with himself; for he is incapable of attaining to the perfection of the heavenly hierarchy. Hooker says, "In the matter of knowledge, there is between the angels of God and the children of men this difference. Angels already have full and complete knowledge in the highest degree that can be imparted unto them; men, if we view them in their spring, are at first without understanding or knowledge at all. Nevertheless, from this utter vacuity they grow by degrees, till they come at length to be even as the angels themselves are. The soul of man being therefore at the first as a book, wherein nothing is, and yet all things may be imprinted, we are to search by what steppes and degrees it riseth unto perfection of knowledge."

Experience teaches that, at different periods of his life, man is unequal in his talents, and advances be slow and progressive steps to such a measure of knowledge as may reward his industry and application. In his infancy, he is little superior to the animals which are void of reason. Light gradually springs up in his mind, and he becomes intelligent. As he advances in years, he learns to know the difference between good and evil, right and wrong. Learning, science, and religion, follow in due course, as the ripening faculties expand; and he may, in the end, by assiduity and research, attain the limited knowledge of which his nature is capable; and this is but to understand and feel his own weakness and incapacity; and humbly to aspire to an increase of light in a better and happier state, through the influence of his religious feelings, and a firm reliance on the aid of that great and perfect Being, who has placed the means of knowledge and happiness within his reach.

The framers of our present system of Freemasonry had some such reference in view when they struck out the comprehensive plan on which it is founded. Its benefits were intended to be progressive; increasing with every step, till it arrived at the great sacrifice of atonement by which we are sanctified, and made capable of a divine inheritance. The first, or blue degrees, are symbolical. They contain no *direct allusion* to the Christian plan of salvation, although the entire system of Craft Masonry is typical of that one event. Every historical landmark is so evident a type of this auspicious scheme, that the coincidence can neither be overlooked nor misapplied. What are the references of Jacob's vision; the three grand offerings; the deliverance from Egyptian bondage; with the burning bush, and the pillar of cloud and of fire; the pot of manna; the scape goat; the brazen serpent; the tabernacle; the ark of the covenant, and its appendages; with many other adjuncts to Blue Masonry, if they are not typical of the Christian dispensation? The whole system is *essentially*, though not *professedly*, Christian.

The reception of these degrees was intended as an exercise of the judgment, and a trial of virtue. The process is gradual, from the rough stone in the north-east angle of the lodge, to the perfected aspirant standing on the five points of fellowship. His progress, however, can only be matured by serious reflection and mental assiduity; without which he will never understand the typical references contained in the degrees he has received, or their tendency to dignify his nature, and make him a wiser and a better man. Still, these steps, sublime though they be, are only preparatory to something infinitely more striking, and more directly applicable to the great dispensation on which all our hopes of happiness, both in this world and a better, are suspended. Red Masonry displays the direct prophecies of the Messiah—the star of Jacob—Shilo—the corner stone—Moses at the bush, &c. In Military Masonry, all these prophecies are fulfiled, and the Christian system clearly developed; while in the Rose Croix, it is displayed in all its comely and perfect proportions.

There are abundant reasons for believing that Freemasonry had not stated lectures before the great revival in 1717; and the disquisitions enjoined at that period were compiled by Drs. Anderson, Desaguliers, and other worthy and learned brethren, from ancient records, and the viva voce information of experienced members of the four old lodges then in active operation. It is evident, from a copy of these primitive lectures in my possession, that the compilers intended to associate Freemasonry, to a certain extent, with Christianity. Thus, at the very outset, in the first degree, we find the candidate assuming to have been recommended by the brethren of the holy lodge of "St John," and professing the Christian doctrine of "ruling and governing his passions, and doing to others as he would have others do to him." He also refers a significant part of the ceremony to an observation of Jesus Christ, "Ask, and ye shall have; seek, and ye shall find; knock, and it shall be opened unto you." They had also a tradition of St. John the Evangelist being invited to take upon himself the Grand Mastership of the Order. Now, although this tradition may be of no authority, yet its very existence proves that our ancient brethren were desirous of connecting Masonry with Christianity by a decided and unequivocal link.

In the lecture of the second degree, we again find a reference to "the Lodge of St. John" and, which is more to our present purpose, we have also an explanation of the Masonic meaning attached to the title "Great Architect of the Universe" who is plainly declared to be Jesus Christ These are the words: "The Grand Architect and Contriver of the Universe, or *He that was taken up to the top of the pinnacle of the Holy Temple*" In another course of lectures, used a few years later, called the "Old York Lectures," we find the five steps in this degree referred to "the birth, life, death, resurrection, and ascension of Jesus Christ." The ceremonies of the third degree were openly explained by learned brethren, not many years after the revival of Masonry, to be typical of Christianity. And it does not weaken the force of the argument, to urge that these direct references were expunged from the system at the revision of the lectures consequent on the Union of Ancient and Modern Masonry in 1813; it is enough to shew that they existed in the earliest known ritual; and hence constitute an evident proof that Freemasonry, at its revival, was considered applicable to that religion which is the perfection of Judaism, and the glory of the whole earth.

I have been led into these observations by the receipt of a letter from an eminent Mason in India, who has obligingly furnished me with some objections against Freemasonry, which appear to be urged with great force and effect in our eastern dependencies, and tend to obstruct the progress of the Order amongst the inhabitants of those distant regions. They are made to assume the form of three separate arguments, and are stated as follows:

1. "It is objected that a true Christian cannot, or ought not, to join in Masonry, because Masons offer prayers to God without the mediation of our Redeemer, through whom alone our prayers can meet with acceptance."

2. "It is objected that we inculcate the principles of brotherly love and charity as peculiarly incumbent on us because we are bound by the ties of Masonry; whereas such acts, to be acceptable to God, should proceed from a love of God, reconciled to mankind through the sacrifice of Christ; any other motive being not only not acceptable, but sinful."

3. "Objects that the mention of the Lord's name in the Lodge is a contravention of the third commandment. It is fully acknowledged that this Name is never introduced with levity, but with the greatest reverence; yet, is not its use in some degree objectionable, in the same way as is its heedless introduction into any ordinary discourse?"

These objections are specious in appearance, but extremely superficial when submitted to the test of critical examination. They all originate in a mistaken idea of the nature and design of Freemasonry. It is assumed to be a system of religion; whereas, in fact, it merely embraces one branch of religion, which is common to all the modes of worshipping God that exist upon the earth. "It is a system of morality, veiled in allegory, and illustrated by symbols." The arguments, therefore, are unsound, and the conclusion groundless; as will appear from a slight examination of their tendency.

1. This objection pronounces it improper to offer up prayers to God without a reference to the mediation of Christ. Now, although prayer is undoubtedly of much greater efficacy when used m the Redeemer's name, yet it will not be difficult to prove that the offering up of such prayers is not without precedent, even amongst the formularies of devotion which have been prescribed for the observance of Christians. Nor will it be necessary to cite the extreme cases of Socinian's and Roman Catholics—the former denying the efficacy of Christ's atonement, and the latter in some cases using the mediation of the Virgin and Saints, in proof of the position. In the Liturgy of our own church, we have no reference to the mediation of Christ in many of the prayers. For instance, in the prayer of St. Chrysostom, they collect for Trinity Sunday, the bishop's prayer in the confirmation service, and, most of all, in that divine prayer which Jesus Christ recommended to his disciples for their daily use. This constitutes an undeniable proof that those pious and holy men who compiled our formularies, did not maintain the exclusive opinion that prayer to God would be unacceptable, even though

under peculiar circumstances, the name of Christ was not directly used.

It may however be demanded of the objectors to verify their assertion, that our prayers have no reference to a Savior; because nothing can be more incorrect; for in all our appeals to God, His Name is actually used, and His mediation implied.

The legitimate prayers of Freemasonry, are short addresses to the GREAT ARCHITECT OF THE UNIVERSE, for a blessing on our labors. Now, who is this divine Being whom we thus invoke? Why, according to the interpretation of our ancient Brethren—"Him that was earned to the top pinnacle of the Holy Temple," or Jesus Christ. Nor is Freemasonry singular in this interpretation. St. Paul says, "Jesus Christ laid the foundations of the earth, and the heavens are the work of his hands;" or in other words that he is the Grand Architect of the Universe. One of our ancient Masonic parallels, St. John says—"All things were made by Him." The Scriptures abound with testimonies to this fact; and as our prayers are all addressed to this glorious Being, I see no force in the objection, although grounded, as it evidently is, on the supposition that Jews, Turks, and Hindoos may join in the prayers, and apply them to the supreme object of their respective adoration. Our ancient Brethren, in the construction of an universal system, have adopted a style in their addresses to the Throne of Grace, which, while it may be undoubtedly applied to the God of the Jews, and Mussulmans, is still more particularly applicable to the Redeemer, under the Christian Covenant, because it is the very title by which he is designated in the inspired writings of the New Testament; and therefore every Christian Mason, in appealing to the Grand Architect of the Universe, ought to be fully impressed with the salutary truth, that his prayer is directed to God, through the mediation of Christ; precisely according to the precedent in the Collects for the third Sunday in Advent, and the first Sunday in Lent, as set forth in the formularies of our Church.

The same reasoning will apply to the Tetragrammaton, or Name of Jehovah, used in the Old Testament, which is universally understood to mean the Messiah or Christ. Some of the Rabbins believe that the Messiah will reveal himself to man by this Name; and our Savior did so; and commanded his disciples to baptize in the name of the Father, Son, and Holy Ghost, which Trinity is comprehended in the name Jehovah. The first letter JOD signifying the Father; the second He, the Son; and the third VAU, the Holy Ghost; the repetition of the letter He referring to the humanity of Christ, as the former He refers to his divinity.

Objection 2. St. Paul's directions to the Galatians on this point are, "*As we have therefore opportunity, let us do good unto all men, especially unto them who are of the household of faith.*" The doctrine of Masonry respecting brotherly love and charity is founded upon this model. "To extend relief to all mankind, especially to those who are brother Masons." In many parts of the Lectures, however, the precepts are general and unrestricted. Thus, at his initiation the candidate is instructed "never to shut his ears against the cries of the distressed, but listening with attention to the recital of their sufferings, pity should flow from his heart accompanied by that relief which their necessities require, and his own circumstances will admit." The definition of Charity contains a similar recommendation. "By the exercise of brotherly love, we are taught to regard the *whole human species* as one family; who, as children of the same parent, and inhabitants of the same planet, are to aid, support, and protect each other." It is unnecessary to multiply examples. The general doctrine pervades the entire system. Indeed, the charge to an E. A. P. confirms it by saying that "the basis on which Freemasonry rests is, *the practice of social and moral virtue, including benevolence and charity.*"

As to the charge of relieving a distressed brother "because he is a Mason," the principle is borne out by the practice of all civilized nations. What are the various asylums, hospitals, benevolent societies, and public charities, but associations for purposes which are exclusive in their operation? The clergy of this country have a fund for the relief of aged and decayed ministers, their widows and orphans, and none other can participate in its bounties. The medical profession, the law, the army and navy possess similar institutions; which indeed are not uncommon amongst other classes of the community. How then can Freemasonry be consistently condemned, because she has her Benevolent Fund for widows, her schools for orphans, and her asylum for worthy aged and decayed Brethren, which are exclusively confined to those for whose benefit they have been peculiarly established? Can a subscription to any of these institutions be offensive to God? Our Savior answers the question in the instructions which he gave to his apostles when he sent them forth to preach the gospel. "Heal the sick, cleanse the lepers, raise the dead, cast out devils; freely you have received, freely give. Into whatsoever city or town ye shall enter, *inquire who in it is worthy*; and there abide till ye go thence. And whosoever shall not receive you nor hear your words, shake off the dust of your feet;" or in other words, withhold from them the benefits of your ministration, and confer them only on those who are worthy.

But it is urged, that "such acts, to be acceptable to God, should proceed from a love of God, reconciled to mankind through the sacrifice of Christ." This argument displays an utter ignorance of the true design of Freemasonry. On the very threshold of the First degree, when the candidate represents the corner-stone of the intended building, the intent of the Order is expounded as a moral edifice of the love of man *founded on the love of God*, and of three great duties linked together, and proceeding from each other, the basis being his duty to, his dependence on, and his reverence for, the Great Architect of the Universe. Nothing can be clearer than this exposition; nothing can more satisfactorily show that in whatever manner we may perform our duty to our neighbor or ourselves, by conferring benefits, all must be founded on a love of God, under the name of the Great Architect of the Universe, which, to the Christian Mason, means Jesus Christ.

Objection 3. To understand this objection rightly, it will be necessary to premise that there are three ways of using the holy Name of God, which have been pronounced sinful. 1. By willful perjury. 2. By rash and profane swearing. 3. By an irreverent use of it in common conversation. It does not appear, however, that either of these is included in the objection, although it is so loosely expressed as to render the precise meaning rather equivocal. The words are—"it is fully acknowledged that this Name is never introduced with levity, but with the greatest reverence. Yet is not its use in some degree objectionable, in the same way as its heedless introduction into any ordinary discourse?" "Now it appears to me that if it be not used in the Lodge with *levity*, it cannot justly be classed with the *heedless* introduction of it into any ordinary discourse." The first application of this Name is not sinful except in its violation. It is introduced into all legal institutions in every part of the world, without the least impropriety. Moses says—"Thou shalt fear the Lord thy God, and shalt swear by his Name." And Bishop Sanderson remarks, "the obligation of an oath ariseth precisely from this, that God is invoked as a witness and avenger. And it is a matter well worthy of the consideration of every man, that as the object of a lawful oath is God alone, so it contains a solemn confession of his omnipresence, his omniscience, and his omnipotence." Apply this reasoning to Freemasonry, and it will appear perfectly justified in the limited use of God's name which prevails in our Lodges.

I am unwilling to believe that the use of the name of the Lord in serious discourse is either sinful or improper. Indeed, I cannot understand how the work of the ministry is to be carried on without it. How is the sinner to be turned from darkness to light,— how are the wicked to be brought to know the error of their ways, if the Redeemer's name is not to be used as an incentive to their reformation. St. James however, is explicit on this point He says, when instructing the Christian converts on the correct method of performing their worldly duties—"Go to now, ye that say, to-day or to-morrow we will go into such a city, and continue there a year, and buy, and sell, and get gain; whereas ye know not what shall be on the morrow. For that *ye ought to say,* IF THE LORD WILL, we shall live, and do this or that." Here is an unexceptionable rule for the use of the Lord's name "in ordinary discourse." It is universally understood, and universally practiced by men of the greatest piety and virtue. It follows, therefore, that its introduction into the serious rituals of Freemasonry is neither unnecessary nor sinful.

I conclude this article with a few apposite remarks from an American publication. "Freemasonry, though constantly assailed, has hitherto remained unhurt by ignorance, superstition, or tyranny; and by the aid of her enlightened philanthropy and undefiled religion, has soared aloft, dipped her broad pencil in the clouds of heaven, and spread the cement of brotherly affection through earth's remotest realms. She has shed her rays in every portion of the habitable globe, and extended her salutary influence to the distressed in every clime. The widow's thanks, and the orphan's tears, are her grateful encomiums. Courtesy and friendship hail her with gratitude. She has promoted the kindly intercourse of nations—she has softened the asperities and diminished the miseries of war—she has smiled upon science and literature; and in concert with other institutions, she has aided Christianity in introducing this distinguished era of light and salvation."

ON THE LANDMARKS OF MASONRY

"Remove not the ancient landmarks, and discover not a secret to another." Solomon.

Our brethren of the last century were so sensitively alive to the necessity of masonic progress, and a judicious amplification of the Lectures, that, within a period of less than sixty years, five improved Rituals were successively produced in England, and received the sanction of Grand Lodge. And they tried the experiment of a Magazine, but the philosophy of Masonry was not sufficiently advanced to insure its success. Their greatest names, however, were influenced by the sound and reasonable principle, that whenever any new lights should be reflected on the institution by important discoveries in natural and inductive science, a partial rearrangement of the Lectures, to embody such improvements as are applicable to the masonic system, might be beneficially adopted; and accordingly, the task was repeated in almost every decade of years, and thankfully accepted by the fraternity.

Indeed, no human science can remain stationary for any length of time without deterioration, and consequent loss of influence: it must either advance or retrograde; it must either substantiate its claims to public estimation, or sink into neglect and contempt. Transition and reproduction are the inevitable destiny of all human institutions. Nothing is absolutely quiescent but the dead; and they are soon forgotten. To prevent Freemasonry from sharing the same fate, there ought to be a periodical revision of the ritual, under the direction of Grand Lodge, every quarter of a century at the least. The example of our brethren in the United States, whose anxiety to promote the social advancement of the Order merits the approval and admiration of all well-disposed brethren in every quarter of the globe, will evince the efficacy and success of such a proceeding, by the large additions which are daily accruing to the number of their lodges and members, and the superior character which the masons of the present day sustain in morals, science and literature, compared with that of the craft only a few years ago, when an anti-masonic cry was raised during the presidential election; and the fiction of Morgan's murder by the craft was successfully propagated by perjury and other unlawful means—sanctioned, alas! by a multitude of unworthy brethren, for the avowed purpose of sweeping the society from the face of the earth.

The doctrine of Progress consists in a disposition to preserve and an ability to improve the social institutions by which mankind are benefited. And who will venture to affirm that such a principle, steadily enunciated, would not augment the influence of Freemasonry? Who will say that the Order would not be in greater request, and produce more lasting benefits to the human race, if its improvements were commensurate with the progress of other sciences which conduce to the general welfare of society? Few will be found to question either of these propositions; and all worthy brethren, who are solicitous to increase its means of doing good, will unite in best wishes for some more genial operation in the working of the system among the English craft; for, although the Order never can become universal, it may, under a proper 'regime', be able to sustain a respectable rank among the moral and scientific societies by which the present age is so illustriously distinguished.

But masonic progress, how necessary and wholesome soever it may be, must not be allowed to overstep those salutary boundaries which our ancient brethren placed, as enduring landmarks, to prescribe the limits of the Order, and point out to future generations that, however prurient might be their zeal and anxiety for internal improvements or organic changes, thus far would they be allowed to expend, their ameliorating exertions, and no further; and it was to effect this purpose, with greater certainty of success, that the landmarks of masonry were originally promulgated, and pronounced unchangeable.

In order to adapt these permanent tokens to the requirements of the masonic institution, they were made applicable to every division and subdivision of its constituent parts, whether appertaining to discipline or doctrine, science or morals, signs, symbols or legends, precept or practice; extending from the most simple elements to the highest mysteries of the craft and they offer such a series of exquisite subjects for amplification, that the instruction which may be legitimately drawn from them alone would serve to illustrate and explain the most comprehensive designs of Masonry.

Definition of a Landmark—The word landmark was used at the revival of Masonry, in 1717, to denote certain standard principles in the general laws, usages, customs and language of the Order, which were originally established by our ancient brethren to preserve his identity and prevent innovation; and it has ever been considered essential to the integrity of Masonry that they should remain intact; because, if its leading tenets were subject to periodical changes, at the will and pleasure of the fraternity in every successive generation, its destructive character, in the process of time, might perchance be destroyed; in which case the institution would be denuded of all its fixed and determinate principles. It was fenced round with landmarks, therefore, to preserve its integrity, and prevent the introduction of unauthorized novelties, which would affect its peculiar claims to consideration in the eye of the world. The question then arises, what are to be considered the landmarks of Masonry which a Grand Lodge is hypothetically incapable of altering? For it is clear that, although, according to the old Charges and Constitutions, laws may be altered by any Grand Lodge, the removal of landmarks is strictly prohibited. And this restriction is perfectly conformable with the exclusive nature of the institution; because, if the landmarks were legitimately changeable. Freemasonry, in the course of time, would lose all its peculiarities by successive innovations, and assume a new character, which the brethren of a former age, who have outlived their half century of masonic experience, would be unable to recognize and unwilling to allow.

It is a question which presents difficulties that have appeared insuperable to many sound-judging members of the craft in all ages; and even in our own, the fraternity are not agreed, either with respect to their number or identity, although, in theory, they are universally admitted to be inaccessible boundaries, which were originally provided to secure the Order from fanciful innovations among its avowed friends, as well as from the inroads of schismatical invasion by its enemies. They may be conveniently classed under the several heads of elementary, inductive, judicial, historical, legislative, ritual or ceremonial, doctrinal and scientific; but great authorities in our own times differ materially in their construction of the tokens by which each class may be distinguished; and it has been found so difficult to arrive at any definite understanding on the subject which is uniformly acceptable to the fraternity, that the same man, under a change of circumstances, will be inclined to acknowledge that for a landmark to-day, which yesterday he would have stoutly affirmed to have been no landmark at all. Nor is this surprising, when we consider, as an opposite analogy, the diversity of opinions which exist among different denominations of Christians respecting the correct interpretation of Scripture, the number and nature of the sacraments, free-will, predestination, and many other abstruse points of doctrine. *De gustibus non est dispuiandum* **(In matters of taste, there can be no disputes)**. The door being thus open to the exercise of private judgment; it becomes extremely difficult to recognize some arcane landmark, and needs a more certain and unerring test than we at present possess to distinguish it correctly.

It would be well if this unsatisfactory state of things could be settled by competent authority, because it is possible that a landmark may be unconsciously violated, and the delinquent arraigned before a judicial board, to answer for a fault of which he is not cognizant, and on which the members themselves may be unable to decide with any degree of precision; for the gist of the investigation would turn upon this pivot, whether the violated rule were really a landmark or not. The question would, doubtless, elicit a diversity of opinions in the committee; and the decision, which would probably be settled by a very small majority, might be ultimately quashed by an adverse judgment in the Grand Lodge.

Great advantages, therefore, would be derived from a declaratory act, distinctly specifying what particular points ought to be received by the fraternity as unalterable landmarks; and such a proceeding would be perfectly conformable with the old law maxim, *nihil magis consentaneum est quam ut usdem modis res dissolvatur quibus constituitur* (**Nothing is more equitable than that everything should be dissolved by the same means by which it was first constituted**). This course, if it were practicable, of which, it is freely admitted, reasonable doubts may be entertained, would terminate all discussion, and set the minds of the brethren at rest on this uncertain and much-contested subject. In the absence of some such proceeding, we will endeavor to ascertain, on the authority of ancient documents, what were considered landmarks by the craft at the earliest period on record, as they were collected and handed down to us in the Lectures which were used during the last century.

OPENING AND CLOSING THE LODGE—To begin with the beginning: The opening and closing of the lodge include many important landmarks, which are absolutely indispensable to the integrity of the Order. For instance, if a lodge be opened in the absence of a stipulated number of brethren; or by any other than the proper officers, and unaccompanied by the prescribed batteries or reports; if this essential ceremony be performed without enumerating the principal and assistant officers, together with a description of their several duties, and including a reference to the cardinal points of the compass; if it be done in an untiled lodge, or without the brethren appearing in order as masons; or if the solemn invocation to T. G. A. O. T. U. be omitted; then the meeting would forfeit the character of a lodge of masons, its transactions would be illegal, and the brethren would become liable to an indictment for irregularity and a violation of the established landmarks. At the closing of the lodge, similar ceremonies have been transmitted to us from the most ancient times, and their observance invests the proceedings with solemnity and decorum; until the members are finally dismissed with an exhortation to fidelity—which is an unchangeable landmark—and they depart in peace, harmony and brotherly love.

The openings in each of the three degrees vary considerably, as is reasonable, and contain their own appropriate landmarks. In the first degree, the lodge is professedly opened "for the purposes of Masonry;" in the second, "on the square, for the instruction and improvement of craftsmen;" in the third, it is opened "on the Center, for the instruction and improvement of master masons;" after having proved the fellow craft by the square, and the master mason by the compasses, and seen that the brethren stand in order, and exhibit demonstrative proofs of their proficiency, the reports being correctly rendered as a marked distinction of the degrees. This is according to the English system. It varies in some trifling particulars from that which is practiced in the United States, but the difference is not very material.

Meet on the Level and Part on the Square.—This landmark was originally introduced into the Lectures, to show that the Order, although confessedly based on the principle of equality, is not the exponent of that species of communism which would destroy rank, equalize property, and reduce society to the common level of a savage state. Nor do its members look forward to the period which was so ardently desired by Condorcet, "when the sun shall shine on none but free men; when a man shall recognize no other master than his reason; when tyrants and their slaves—when priests, together with their stupid and hypocritical agents, will have no further existence but in history or on the stage." It is only when the lodge is open that the brethren, without any reference to a diversity of rank, are equal; and during the process of working the Lectures, each bears the burden assigned to him by the Master for the furtherance of that common object, the acquisition of knowledge. But having met on the level, they part on the square. When the lodge is closed, and the jewels put by, each individual resumes his rank in society, and honor is given where honor is due. A practical illustration is thus afforded of that divine precept, "by this shall all men know that ye are my disciples, if ye love one another." This is the true and only principle on which the general business of Masonry is conducted—"innocence being its characteristic, and peace and good-will to man its only end and aim."

CONCERNING CANDIDATES—By studying the landmarks, an industrious brother will acquire an accurate knowledge of the boundaries within which his investigations ought to be confined. And for want of some such incipient training, many a zealous mason has abandoned the Order in despair. There is one rule respecting candidates which every brother ought to understand distinctly, as an inalienable landmark in Masonry: that no one can under any circumstances, invite his friend to become a mason, because a disappointed candidate would then have it in his power to say that he had been inveigled into the Order for the sake of the fee; which would bring upon it a scandal, rather than a benefit. Every person who offers himself for initiation is, therefore, bound by another stringent landmark, which the Grand Lodge of England has invested with the authority of a law, solemnly to declare that he has not been biased by the solicitations of friends, or by any mercenary or other unworthy motive; and that his request for admission is made from a favorable opinion of the institution, and a desire of knowledge. Thus, in the beautiful language of the Lectures, he must freely and voluntarily ask, if he would have; seek, if he would find; and knock, if he wishes the door of Masonry to be opened for his admission into the Order.

After this avowal, if the revelations of Masonry be not to his taste, and the instruction which he receives does not realize his anticipations, the fault will rest entirely with himself, and the institution will be blameless. Such a result, however, is of a very infrequent occurrence; for where the initiation has been well conducted, and the candidate is made to understand the true nature and reasonableness of the elementary rites, expressions of dissatisfaction or regret are not often heard. But it cannot be denied that if, on the other hand, the W. Master is incompetent; if he performs the ceremonies in a slovenly and inaccurate manner, and omit the usual luminous explanations; if he be so inconsiderate as to hurry them over, in anticipation of the banquet that is to follow (forgetting that the candidate might enjoy a public supper without being made a mason, if he were so inclined); and oblivious to the fact that hard drinking and late hours rather tend to disgust than gratify a great proportion of our candidates—the newly-initiated brother might be tempted to doubt the propriety of customs which present an undignified appearance, foreign to the presumed solemnity of the occasion; and under this mistaken idea, decline the offer of a second and third degree.

Such an abandonment of Masonry on the threshold, however, would be unjust to the fraternity; for a candidate, how talented soever he might be, would be altogether incompetent to form a correct opinion of the society's real tendency, from such a casual and imperfect view as a first impression might create. He must carefully mark, learn, and inwardly digest his acquisitions, for a long period before he undertakes to pronounce a decisive judgment upon them; and it indicates a weak and unstable mind to be deterred by the first obstacle that may present itself. Common prudence would suggest that when a candidate has paid his admission-fee, he should be at some pains to examine the article which has been put into his hands in return for his money, and to ascertain whether it be of an adequate value. If he receives a gem, and casts it from him without inquiry, the fault, as well as the loss, will be his own, and the society from which he received it cannot reasonably be answerable for the consequences. When thus deserted by an incurious brother, the regret of the fraternity is exhausted after they have bid him God speed.

ADMISSION OF CANDIDATES—To prevent disappointments of this nature from being of frequent occurrence, another landmark directs the brethren of a lodge to proceed with great deliberation in the admission of candidates, by making a strict perquisition, before the ballot is taken, into the character they sustain among their neighbors and friends. This may be ascertained with sufficient accuracy by a careful examination of their antecedents, and the testimony of those with whom they have been connected in the affairs of business or the pursuits of pleasure. The most ancient landmarks that we are acquainted with provide that "the son of a bondman shall not be admitted as an apprentice, lest his introduction into the lodge should cause dissatisfaction among the brethren;" and that the candidate must be of good morals, without blemish, and have the full and proper use of his limbs; for "a maimed man," as the York Constitutions express it, "can do the craft no good." By the assistance of these plain and simple directions, added to others which have been subsequently enjoined by Speculative Grand Lodges, no difficulty can arise in estimating the qualifications of a candidate for initiation.

If he be found eligible, and has acquired an unsullied reputation for honesty, sobriety, quietness of demeanor, and teachableness of disposition, he will be welcomed into the lodge with acclamations and a cordial greeting; but if, on the other hand, he has been systematically unjust in his dealings, uncertain in his temper, and of groveling or impure habits—easily susceptible of offence, and addicted to sarcastic recrimination or intemperate remarks—let the fraternity beware how they admit such a person among them; for he will assuredly convert the harmony and brotherly love which ought always to be the prevailing characteristic of a mason's lodge, into a bear garden of dispute and unbrotherly attack—of loud harangue and passionate reply.

THE BALLOT—Every facility is afforded for making the necessary inquiries. The laws and landmarks equally provide that, before a candidate can be admitted, he must be proposed in an open lodge, and a notice to that effect served on each individual member in the ensuing summons, with his name, occupation, and place of abode, distinctly specified. And to afford ample time for deliberate investigation, the ballot cannot legally be taken, except in cases of emergency, till the next regular lodge-night; when, if approved, the candidate may receive the first degree; because it is presumed that every brother, before he records his vote, has made due inquiry, and is perfectly satisfied that the candidate possesses the necessary qualifications to become a good and worthy mason.

PREPARATION—Every existing institution is distinguished by some preliminary ceremony of admission, which is inaccessible to those who are unable to establish an indisputable claim to participate in its privileges. The approved candidate in Freemasonry having sought in his mind and asked of his friend, its tiled door is now about to be opened and its secrets disclosed. The preparation is accompanied by ceremonies which, to a superficial thinker, may appear trifling and undignified, although they embody a series of references to certain sublime matters, which constitute the very essence of the institution, and contribute to its stability and permanent usefulness, if, in accordance with the advice of St. Paul, everything be done decently and in order. But ceremonies, considered abstractedly, are of little value, except as they contribute their aid to impress upon the mind scientific beauties and moral truths. And this is the peculiar characteristic of Freemasonry, which, although its rites and observances are studiously complicated throughout the whole routine of its consecutive degrees, does not contain a single ceremony that is barren of intellectual improvement; for they all bear a direct reference to certain ancient usages recorded in the Book, which is always expanded on the pedestal in the East.

The ceremonies appropriate to the preparation of a candidate for Masonry are designed to impress upon his mind, by an association of ideas, a series of inductive landmarks, both doctrinal and historical, which it is necessary that he should comprehend and permanently remember. The actual preparation is of two kinds, internal and external. But the latter is of the greatest importance, because it constitutes the chief elementary landmark, which renders a candidate perfectly eligible for admission into the sacred tabernacle of a lodge. Before such eligibility can be attained, he is solemnly admonished that a lodge is a place where peace, harmony and brotherly love flourish in their greatest purity; where all wrangling and quarreling, slander and backbiting are strictly prohibited, and therefore nothing offensive or defensive is allowed to enter; because, as the former is forbidden by the old Charges and Constitutions of Masonry, the latter is, of course, unnecessary. This wise precaution is used to typify the perfect moral equality which exists among the brethren in open lodge, where worldly wealth, social rank or political distinction are of no value, either in procuring admission or acquiring the character of a bright mason; and further, to point out, as worthy of recollection, a particular arrangement which was used with such beneficial effect at the building of King Solomon's Temple, as to make it the most noble structure than existing in the world for riches, magnificence and glory.

Such a result could not have been accomplished in the absence of certain stringent regulations which were adopted among the workmen in the forest, the quarries and the casting ground; and by the observance of which the members of every lodge were devoted to an exclusive service, under circumstances that might easily test the accuracy or detect the imperfections of each man's work. Under this arrangement the stones were hewn, carved and prepared for use, in the extensive quarries of Zeredatha, and carefully marked and numbered by officers appointed for that especial purpose. The same process was adopted in the forest of Lebanon; and when the timber was made ready, it was, in like manner, marked and numbered also. The materials were then embarked on floats or rafts, and landed at the seaport town of Joppa, and from thence conveyed on carriages of wood to Jerusalem. Being thus artistically prepared, they were put together in a scientific manner without the intervention of either axe, hammer or metal tool, to prevent the pollution of that sacred edifice. The excellence of the craft in those days was thus substantially vindicated; for, although the stones and timber were hewn and prepared at SO great a distance, yet when put together on Mount Moriah, each part fitted with such perfect exactness, that it appeared to be the work of T, Gr. A. O. T. U., rather than an exertion of human skill.

There are other ceremonies used during this preliminary process of equal importance, which constitute immovable landmarks, and are essential to the integrity of the Order. For instance, if a physical contignation be intercepted between any object and the human eye, it will necessarily prevent that object from being visible, although the understanding remains actively awake; and it is no uncommon circumstance for the heart to conceive before the eye is permitted to discover any peculiar secrets, the premature revelation of which might be extremely prejudicial. Much better would it be—if a candidate display any indisposition to undergo the accustomed ceremonies, or to comply with the constitutional requisitions of the Order—much better would it be that he should quit the lodge, without being favored with an opportunity of discovering its form; for it is a paramount duty incumbent on every good mason—and bad one too—to keep all the world in ignorance respecting the arcane mysteries of the institution, until the privilege be worthily attained and legitimately conferred; in compliance with another ancient landmark, which enjoins that "every Apprentice shall keep his Master's council, and not betray the secrets of his lodge."

And this is not all; for the preparation embraces certain figurative representations of the virtues of confidence, sincerity, humility and fidelity, by a mystical reference to the arms, breast, knees and feet; all of great importance in the system of Freemasonry, as they inculcate the practice of universal beneficence, and instruct the candidate to be as eyes to the blind and feet to the lame; and whenever in his progress through life, he meets with a worthy man, and particularly a mason, in a state of unavoidable distress, to extend freely the right hand of fellowship to comfort, succor and protect him.

THE BADGE—In the lodges of the last century, some trifling varieties existed in the arrangements during the process of initiation; for a perfect uniformity, however desirable, had not been attained. To explain them here would be superfluous, and perhaps not altogether prudent. Suffice it to say, that in some lodges the investiture took place before the candidate was entrusted with the peculiar secrets of the degree, while others practiced a formula similar to that which was enjoined at the Union in 1813. The Senior Warden performed the duty, and recommended the candidate to wear the apron as a badge of innocence and bond of friendship, in the full assurance that if he never disgraced that badge, it would never disgrace him. It will be unnecessary to extend this article, as an elaborate exposition of the landmark may be found in the Signs and Symbols, Lecture X. There are other elementary landmarks embodied in the initiation, but they are so well known and generally understood, that it will scarcely be necessary to enumerate them, much less to go into the detail of a particular illustration, which indeed would be unauthorized, and constitute, if not a legal offence against the Constitutions of Masonry, at least a moral infringement of the O. B.

TESTS OF INDUSTRY—Every candidate at his initiation, should carefully note the particulars of the ceremony; and if there should happen to be some things which appear to his inexperience unnecessary, and others that he cannot exactly comprehend, he may conceive it to be within the bounds of probability that they will admit of a satisfactory explanation. For it is scarcely to be supposed, even by the most obtuse intellect, that in the nineteenth century educated men would meet together periodically to waste their time in unprofitable discussions; to lend the sanction of their names to propagate a fiction, or to engage in pursuits which lead to no advantageous result. Let the candidate use the means at his disposal to remove all false impressions, by studying his elementary exercise—the tests of the first degree, which are enjoined by the authority of many Grand Lodges—and ought to be by all—as a proof of his industry, and a desire of knowledge; for they are intended to convey some preliminary insight into our allegorical system.

It needs no extended argument to prove that the only certain method of attaining excellence in any liberal art or science, is to commence with first principles. To acquire the art of reading, we must begin with the alphabet; and the theory of any trade can only be attained by a preliminary knowledge of its technical terms and phrases. Divinity and science have their catechisms, and Freemasonry its tests, which in England are called Qualification Questions, and contain a simple but comprehensive digest of certain fundamental elements that show the nature and bearing of each advancing degree, and include within a small compass the greatest possible amount of information on all its essential points. Some of the most prominent landmarks are alluded to in these tests; and it is esteemed a *sine qua non* (**An essential condition; a thing that is absolutely necessary.**) for every candidate, while passing through the degrees, to make himself acquainted with them, that he may acquire a correct idea of the nature and tendency of the institution, and be thus prepared for the expansion of the system which is to follow; for there is not a single rite or ceremony, however minute, that does not embody some highly important precept or doctrine, which the candidate may beneficially reduce to practice in his commerce with the world.

These tests are of much greater importance than is generally imagined, because they are intended to constitute the leading feature of Masonry in the mind of a newly initiated member; and in lodges where, unfortunately, they are disregarded, and passed over as matters of little moment. Freemasonry is no better than a common club, and is not worth the time and expense that are bestowed upon it. It would be well if the compendium contained in these preliminary examinations formed a portion of the exercises of every lodge at its opening, because whatever is worth doing at all is worth doing well. It is to be feared, however, that in many of our lodges the candidates are allowed to travell through all the degrees without ever hearing that such a formula is in existence. And even where it is used, the questions in different lodges vary so essentially, that a brother initiated in our lodge, how perfect soever he may be in its tests, will find himself embarrassed by the interrogatories of another. Hence, great advantages would undoubtedly arise, if every Grand Lodge were to enjoin on its subordinates the use of an authorized formula, which they were forbidden to change.

THE GREAT PLAN OF HUMAN SALVATION TRACED IN FREEMASONRY
BY THE LIGHT OF ONE OF ITS MOST PROMINENT SYMBOLS

The abundance of Christian types which are dispersed throughout the entire system of speculative freemasonry must have a tendency to show that the Order is essentially Christian. In its earliest stages, it was undoubtedly a patriarchal and Jewish institution; but, like the design of the Mosaical economy, its reference was evidently to a better dispensation, which had been promised to Adam at the fall, and renewed to all the principal patriarchs in succession; revealed to the prophets, and perfected at the Advent of Christ. The principal types which have been recorded in Holy Scripture, are incorporated into the system of Freemasonry, and constitute landmarks which are unchangeable. The conclusion, therefore, is evident. If they are types of the Redeemer in one instance, they must be also in the other. And as the Jewish religion was a temporary dispensation to herald a more perfect system of faith, so Jewish Freemasonry was the precursor and symbol of that which is now Christian.

One of the most remarkable of these types is that luminous appearance which enlightens the center of our Lodges, called the Blazing Star.

This ornament refers to the sun; and is considered by Masons to be an emblem of Prudence. Thus, our lectures say: "The Blazing

Star, or glory in the center, refers us to that grand luminary the sun, which enlightens the earth, and by its genial influence, dispenses blessings to mankind." And again, "It is placed in the center, ever to be present to the eye of the Mason, that his heart may be attentive to the dictates, and steadfast in the laws of prudence; for prudence is the rule of all virtues; prudence is the path which leads to every degree of propriety; prudence is the channel whence self-approbation forever flows; she leads us forth to worthy actions; and, as a Blazing Star, enlightens us through the dreary and darksome paths of life." But the Masons of the last century applied this symbol in a sense much more appropriate and sublime. It was said to represent "the star which led the wise men to Bethlehem, proclaiming to mankind the nativity of the Son of God, and here conducting our spiritual progress to the author of our Redemption." And this application of the symbol is blended with the former by our transatlantic Brethren thus, "The Blazing; Star is emblematical of that prudence which ought to appear conspicuous in the conduct of every Mason; but more especially commemorative of the star which appeared in the east to guide the wise men to Bethlehem, and proclaim the birth and the presence of the Son of God."

This latter reference of the Blazing Star it will be my purpose to illustrate in the present article.

St. John speaks of the sublime being who was thus proclaimed, under the name of the WORD. In Freemasonry, he is denominated as the Great Architect of the Universe, which has precisely the same significance. Tertullian says "God made the fabric of this world out of nothing by means of his WORD, Wisdom, or Power." The ancient philosophers held the opinion that the Word or Wisdom was the creator of all things; and Zeno plainly terms him the Great Architect of the Universe. The doctrine of the inspired Evangelist could not therefore, be misunderstood, when he said, "In the beginning was the Word, and the Word was with God, and the Word was God. All things were made by him; and without him was not anything made that was made. In him was life; and the life was the light of man. And the light shineth in darkness; and the darkness comprehended it not. And the Word was made flesh, and dwelt among us."

There is an old tradition amongst Masons that this passage was in existence long before St. John flourished; and that, finding the formula suited to his purpose, he commenced his evangelical labors with it. Henry O'Brien says, "That St. John never wrote them, is beyond all question; but having found them to his hand, existing after the circuit of ages and centuries, the composition seemed so pure, and so consonant with Christianity, nay, its very vitality and soul, he adopted it as the preface to his own production." In the English system of Freemasonry, this tradition is exploded; but it is retained in all other parts of the world. It is mentioned by several credible authors in early times of Christianity; and we are quite sure that our ancient Brethren attached to it this precise signification. Thus, it is related by Philostorgius, and after him by Nicephorus, that at the clearing of the foundations, when Julian the apostate set himself to rebuild the temple, a stone was taken up that covered the mouth of a deep square cave, cut out of the rock, into which one of the laborers, being let down by a rope, found in the center of the floor a cubical pillar, on which lay a roll or book, wrapped up in a fine linen cloth, which being unfolded was found to contain, amongst other matter, the commencement of the Gospel of St. John, in capital letters, In the beginning was the Word, &c.

The expression "in the beginning was the Word" evidently referred to the pre-existence and eternity of Christ, because St. John glances at times, not only prior to the incarnation, but to the creation of the world. In the system of Freemasonry propounded by Scroeder, a tedious and abstruse philosophical lecture concludes with asserting that this Word was, and is, and forever shall be, the noble tree, and spiritual philosopher's stone, even Christ Jesus the "Lord." This Word was termed Light, one of the primitive names of our science. Again, he says, "the Word was with God;" or, was of one substance with the Father; as he himself declares when he says, "I and my Father are one." The same was in the beginning with God, and united with the Father from all eternity; which is expressed in the Apocalypse by **A** and **Ω** and originated the nineteenth degree of the Rite *Ancien et Accepte* called Grand Pontiff. "All things were made by Him." He was the Creator and Grand Architect of the Universe, so to in Freemasonry, and symbolized by a blazing star; and the words "was made flesh and dwelt among men," are an illustration of the star personified.

The evidences of this fact are numerous and striking. When any great event for the benefit of mankind has been deemed necessary, it has been invariably effected by the agency of the Great Architect of the Universe, manifested in a visible lucid appearance, as a smoke, a cloud, a fire, or a Mazing star. Hence Philo terms the divine Word, "a supercelestial star." All the various revelations of the Deity, whether in the works of creation, providence, or redemption, were made through him, and therefore, he is properly styled the Word of God. He conversed with Adam in the garden of Eden and the appearance was uniformly by a light like fire; appeared after the fall as a *flaming sword*; fell like *a beam of glory* upon Abel's sacrifice; passed like the *flaming of a lamp* between the sacrifices of Abraham; displayed himself in *the pillar of a cloud and a fir*, which guided and protected the Israelites in their deliverance from Egyptian bondage; in the cloud of glory, and in the judgment of Urim. The same being appeared under such different forms as were best adapted to the occasion–to Abraham under the oak of Mamre; and the Chaklee paraphrast to express that "God went up from Abraham," uses the words *Fulgur Déi*; to Isaac at Beersheba; to Jacob at Mahanaim; to Moses, as a flame of fire, at Horeb; and to Joshua before the city of Jericho; he answered the prayers of Elijah by *fire*; and those of Solomon, at the dedication of the temple, by the same element.

But the most remarkable manifestation of the Grand Architect of the Universe, is that which is symbolized in Freemasonry by a Blazing Star, is the herald of our salvation. We have already seen that almost every appearance, from the creation to the advent of Christ, was attended with a luminous appearance like fire, or the flame of a lamp; therefore, the star in the east, which was seen by the wise men, would be of the same nature; for when it appeared, they immediately departed, and it conducted them on their way to Bethlehem, "till it came and stood over the place where the young child was." It was the same *glory of the Lord* which, on the night of the nativity, shone round about the pious shepherds near Bethlehem; and might, therefore, have been of a globular form, and ascending along with the celestial choir, might have been seen in its ascent by the magi at the distance of five or six hundred miles, diminished to the size of a star, hovering over the land of Judea. This appearance must have strongly attracted their notice and attention. And if these magi were the descendants of Balaam, who prophesied of the star to rise out of Jacob, and also of the school of Daniel, who foretold the precise time of the coming of Messiah, we may naturally account for their journey to Jerusalem; which is illustrated in a Masonic degree called the Illustrious Order of the Cross; and their adoration of the divine child who was a light to lighten the Gentiles, and a glory to his people Israel;" the day-spring from on high; the bright and morning star; the day-star which riseth in our hearts.

Chalcidius in his commentary on the Timæus of Plato, corroborates this opinion declaring it to be "the universal belief of all nations that the appearance of a certain star should declare the descent of a venerable Deity for the salvation of mankind." And he adds; "When this star had been seen by some truly wise men amongst the Chaldeans who were well versed in the contemplation of the heavenly bodies, they made enquiry concerning the birth of God; and when they had found him, they paid him the worship and adoration which were due to so great a being."

The final manifestation of the Great Architect of the Universe is recorded in the ingenious degree of Knight of the East and West, taken from the book of Revelation. "And I saw heaven opened, and behold, a white horse; and he that sat upon him was called Faithfull and True; and in righteousness he doth judge and make war. His eyes were as a *flame of fire*, and on his head were many crowns; and he had a name written that no man knew but he himself. And he was clothed with a vesture dipped in blood; and his name is called the Word of God. And the armies which were in heaven followed him upon white horses, clothed in fine linen, white and clean. And out of his mouth goeth a sharp sword, that with it he should smite the nations; and he shall rule them with a rod of iron; and he treadeth the winepress of the fierceness and wrath of Almighty God. And he hath on his vesture and on his thigh a name written. KING OF KINGS, AND LORD OF LORDS."

Now considering the omnipresent nature of God, that the heaven of heavens cannot contain him, he necessarily fills all space, and extends through all extent, connecting earth, heaven, and every part of the universe, in a chain of endless gradation; expressed in Freemasonry under the symbol of "a circle whose center is everywhere, and whose circumference is nowhere." Whether we contemplate the most minute or the most magnificent objects of the creation, our minds are filled with an equal degree of wonder, awe, and adoration. All is Masonry. The spacious firmament, containing those blazing stars which beautify and adorn the spangled *canopy of heaven*, was the work of his hands; nor could the smallest particle of dust have been produced but by his holy word. It was the Great Architect of the Universe whom God employed in forming the universe out of nothing; and the same Almighty Being is used in supporting and governing his own workmanship; and the visible communications vouchsafed by God to man, are referred by St. Paul to Jesus Christ, who, he says, "*being the brightness of his glory*" and the express image of his person, and upholding all things by the word of his power when he had by himself purged our sins, sat down on "the right hand of the majesty on high."

St. Paul uses the word ANATOLE, *Oriens*, to represent the Redeemer of mankind in his glorious brightness. In the application of this word, some distinctions have been made: means, from the east; by the rising of stars in general is signified; and by the expression of St. Luke, the rising of a particular star in the east, which is the blazing star of Freemasonry, and, with the Cabalists, denoted the eternal wisdom of God which is the same as the eternal WORD of God, or Christ. And hence the early Christians, when they prayed, turned their eyes towards the east, or in other words, towards the Savior, who was crucified with his face towards the west. Clemens Alexandrinus gives as a reason for praying towards the east, that it is the dayspring, or source of light. And the same practice constitutes an essential ceremony in our Lodges, where wisdom is placed in the east.

God created man upright, in mind as well as in body; but he was tempted by the serpent to fall into sin, which was immediately punished. He was driven out of the happy garden, and the Shekinah, or blazing star from heaven, was placed as a guard to protect the tree of life. From this, Shekinah proceeded that celebrated cabalistical symbol of the Deity called the Sephiroth, consisting of ten splendors, three of which are placed as the united light of God, or crown of glory. They were called splendors from a Hebrew root, signifying that they shone with the brightness of the sapphire. "*Corona Jtumma, que est mysterium centri, ipsa est radix abscondita, et tres menteg superiores sunt germen, quae uniunt sese in centro, quod est radix earum; septem vero numerationes qus sunt rami, uniunt se germini quod refert mentes, et omnes se uniunt in centro, quod est radix in mysterio nominis radicalis et essentialis, qus radix influit in omnes et unit omnes influentia sua.*" (**The crown of the Jtumma, which is the mystery of the center, it is the root that is hid and the higher they are, the branch of the three menteg, which are uniting themselves in the center, that is the root of their true Wills; Seven numbering losing their branches, one in the spring and reports minds and they all combine in the center, which is the root of a secret radical and essential for losing a root flow into the unit and they all influence.**) In one of the ineffable degrees of Masonry, called "Master in Israel," the blazing star is made to consist of five points, like a royal crown, in the center of which appears the initial of the sacred name. They refer to the five equal lights of Masonry, *viz.*, the Bible, square, compasses, key, and triangle; and as the blazing star enlightens the physical, so the five equal points should enlighten the moral condition of an initiated Brother. They denoted the five orders of architecture; the five points of fellowship; the five senses, which constitute the physical perfection of man; and the five zones of the world, all of which are masonically peopled.

The punishment of Adam was followed by repentance, and repentance was the basis of that covenant between God and man, which is embodied in the system of speculative Masonry; and comprehends the promise of salvation through faith in a Redeemer, who should bruise the serpent's head. Hence, the serpent has been introduced amongst our symbols. One of M. Peuvret's degrees refers to this event: but it is expressed so cabalistically obscure as to be difficult of comprehension. Thus, the lecture says, "When Adam was created, the light of his life shone in the pure oil of divine essentiality; but, by his fall, mortal water penetrated so that his mercury became a cold poison, which was before an exaltation to joyfulness. So came darkness into his oil, and he died to the divine light, drawn thereto by the property of the serpent; for in the serpent the wrath kingdom and outward also was manifest, whose subtilty Eve desired." With much more of the same kind.

The conditions of the divine covenant included repentance, faith and obedience, or our duty to God, our neighbor, and ourselves. And this was primitive Freemasonry. In different ages and nations, the rites and ceremonies of religious worship varied; but its essence was always the same wherever the worship of the true God prevailed. And even when it was abandoned the factious worship of the spurious Freemasonry was so modelled as to imitate it as nearly as human reason could approach divine perfection. The principal feature in primitive worship, as in dl succeeding ages till the coming of Christy, was annual sacrifices, instituted as an atonement for sin, and typical of that one great sacrifice offered by Jesus Christ as an expiation for the sins of all mankind. This sacrifice is not obscurely intimated in Freemasonry; but several of the degrees are founded upon, and derive all their excellence from, the awful fact. In Templarism is described, "the splendid conclusion of the hallowed sacrifice, offered by the Redeemer of mankind, to propitiate the anger of an offended Deity." And again, in another degree, the Senior Sir Knight is directed to "take the signet, and set a mark on the forehead of those who have passed through tribulation patiently, and have washed their robes, and have made them white in the blood of the Lamb which was slain, from the foundation of the world." The Thrice Illustrious Order of the Cross thus notices the atonement: "It is now the first hour of the day, the time when our Lord suffered, and the veil of the temple was rent in sunder; when darkness and consternation was spread over the earth; and when the confusion of the old covenant was made light in the new, in the temple of the cross." There are several other Masonic degrees in which the crucifixion is referred to, and particularly the Rose and Prince of the Royal Secret.

The system of religion, or Lux, or Masonry, call it by what name you will, was practiced by the first family after the unhappy fall of man; and God's acceptance of Abel's sacrifice proves that his Freemasonry was true, and that his faith in obtaining salvation through the promised Messiah, and his obedience resulting from it, were well pleasing in the sight of God, for "he obtained witness that he was righteous." This distinction tempted Cain to forfeit his obligation, and wrought upon the stormy passions of his heart till he murdered his brother, and fled into the land of Nod. Hence originated the degree called the Knight of the Black Mark. In his new residence he founded a colony, built a fortified city, and laid the basis of that idolatry, which was subsequently embodied in the spurious Freemasonry, and soon overspread and contaminated the world. Amidst the accumulating oblivion of religious knowledge, Enodi, a primitive Mason, held the faith of the promised Messiah. "By faith Enoch was translated, that he should not see death; and was not found, because God had translated him; for before his translation he bad this testimony, that he pleased God." He clearly evinced his faith in Christ Jesus; and displayed a knowledge of his first coming by prophesying of his second. "Behold," says he, "the Lord cometh with ten thousand of his saints, to execute judgment upon all; and to convince all that are ungodly among them, of all their ungodly deeds which they have ungodly committed, and of all their hard speeches which ungodly sinners have spoken against him."

ON FREEMASONRY

I have often wondered how it could happen that our forefathers, the Freemasons of England, should have omitted to work out the details of Masonry in a more particular and perfect manner than we find it accomplished in the publications of the last century; although it was generally believed, even then, that such discussions were extremely advantageous to the Order, being calculated to dissipate the mists and prejudices which biased the minds of men, and indisposed them for the reception of truth. Numerous evidences of this fact are scattered over the writings of the few Masonic authors, which distinguished that period. "The best way," says Laurie, in his preface, "of refuting the calumnies which have been brought against the fraternity of Freemasons, is to lay before the public a correct and rational account of the nature, origin, and progress of the institution, that they may be enabled to determine whether or not its principles are, in any shape, connected with the principles of revolutionary anarchy, and whether or not the conduct of its members has ever been similar to the conduct of traitors." And from the publication of such sentiments, it must be evident to every Brother's experience, that the feeling against Freemasonry, which displayed itself so openly only a few years ago, has assumed a much milder form, if it be not entirely removed.

It will not, however, be difficult to account for the dearth of Masonic writers in a preceding age. Before the eighteenth century, symbolical Masonry had no lectures; and, consequently, while it was confined to a simple ceremonial, needed no illustrations; because, as the science was chiefly operative, the secrets would be those which had a reference to building, to the scientific ornaments and decorations of each particular style of architecture as it flourished in its own exclusive period, and these mysteries were communicated gradually, as the candidate rose through the different stages of his order or profession.

There appears to have been one general principle which extended itself over every style from the early English to the florid, decorated, and perpendicular, and constituted one of the most ineffable secrets of the Masonic Lodges. It is now known to have been the hieroglyphical device styled *vesica piscis*; "Which may be traced from the church of St. John Lateran, and old St. Peter's at Rome, to the church at Bath, one of the latest Gothic buildings of any consequence in England. It was formed by two equal circles, cutting each other in their centers, and was held in high veneration, having been invariably adopted by Master Masons in all countries. In bas-reliefs, which are seen in the most ancient churches, over doorways, it usually circumscribes the figure of our Savior. It was indeed a principle which pervaded every building dedicated to the Christian religion, and has been exclusively attributed to a knowledge of Euclid."

The prevailing secrets of the Lodges in these early times, were the profound dogmata of Geometry and Arithmetic, by the use of which all their complicated designs were wrought out and perfected. These sciences are inseparable from the system; and accordingly, hare been faithfully transmitted to our own times. "The secret meetings of the Master Masons," says Dallaway, "within a particular district, were confined to consultations with each other, which mainly tended to the communication of science, and of improvement in their art. An evident result was seen in the general uniformity of their designs in architecture, with respect both to plan and ornament, yet not without deviations. We may conclude that the craft or mystery of architects and operative masons was involved in secrecy, by which a knowledge of their practice was carefully excluded from the acquirement of all who were not enrolled in their fraternity. Still, it was absolutely necessary that when they engaged in contracts with bishops, or patrons of ecclesiastical buildings, a specification should be made of the component parts, and of the terms by which either contracting party should be rendered conversant with them. A certain nomenclature was then divulged by the Master Masons for such a purpose, and became in general acceptation in the Middle Ages."

The abstruse calculations, which accompanied the sciences of geometry and arithmetic, are no longer necessary to Freemasonry, as an institution purely speculative; and they were accordingly omitted in the revised system as it was recommended to the notice of the fraternity by the Grand Lodge in 1717, and we retain only the beautiful theory of these sciences, with their application to the practice of morality, founded on the power and goodness of the G. A. O. T. U. in the construction of the system in which we live.

It would be an injustice to our Brethren of the last century to believe that they did not entertain a profound veneration for the principles of the Masonic Order. But the customs and habits of the people of England living in that day, differed materially from our own. There were times when conviviality and a love of social harmony prevailed over the more sedate pursuits and investigations of science in which such an astonishing progress distinguishes me in present times. In the seventeenth and eighteenth centuries London was an atmosphere of clubs, and a society of this kind existed in every street for the peculiar use of its inhabitants, besides those which were exclusively frequented by persons possessing similar tastes or habits of amusement. And it will be no disparagement to Masonry, if we believe that its private Lodges did not sustain a much higher rank than some of these celebrated meetings; for the Kit Cat, the Beefsteak, and other clubs, were frequented by the nobility and most celebrated literary characters of that polished era.

It was the organization of Freemasonry that gave it the distinctive character which elevated its pretensions above the common routine of club life; and although it is admitted that the members of the latter entertained a strong attachment to their several institutions, yet none were so enthusiastic as those who had enlisted in the cause of Masonry as we may learn from the few testimonies which remain. A Mason of high standing, a hundred years ago, thus expresses his feelings respecting the Order. "Masonry is the daughter of heaven; and happy are those who embrace her. By it, youth is passed over without agitation, the middle age without anxiety, and old age without remorse. Masonry teaches the way to content, a thing almost unknown to the greatest part of mankind. In short, its ultimate resort is to enjoy in security the things that are to reject all meddlers in state affairs or religion, or of a trifling nature; to embrace those of real moment and worthy tendency, with fervency and zeal unfeigned as sure of being unchangeable as ending in happiness. They are rich without riches intrinsically possessing all desirable goods; and have the less to wish for by the enjoyment of what they have. Liberty, peace and tranquility, are the only objects worthy of their diligence and trouble."

But this, as well as almost all the testimonies of that period to its superior excellence, is confined exclusively to morals.

Modern revision has however extended the limits of scientific investigation in the Order of Freemasonry beyond what was intended by those who decreed that "the privileges of Masonry should no longer be restricted to operative Masons, but extend to men of various professions, provided they were regularly approved and initiated into the Order." And Dr. Hemming and his associates, at the Union in 1813, thought it expedient to add some peculiar disquisitions from the system of Pythagoras, on the combinations of the point, the line, the superficies, and the solid, to form rectangular, trilateral, quadrilateral, multilateral figures, and the regular bodies; the latter of which, on account of their singularity, and the mysterious nature usually ascribed to them, were formerly known by the name of the five Platonic bodies; and they were so highly regarded by the ancient Geometricians, that Euclid is said to have composed his celebrated work on the Elements, chiefly for the purpose of being able to display some of their most remarkable properties.

These disquisitions usually conclude with an explanation of the forty-seventh problem of Euclid, which is called the Eureka of Pythagoras.

Our transatlantic Brethren have improved upon this still further. Some of the Grand Lodges have given a public sanction to the introduction of literary and scientific subjects, not contained in the usual lectures, and the open discussion of them at the private meetings of the society. And a committee of the Grand Lodge of New York, in their report for the year 1842, decided that "Masonic periodicals, if judiciously conducted, are calculated to accomplish a vast amount of good, by diffusing more extensively those sound, moral, and benevolent principles, which so eminently characterize this venerable institution; your committee, therefore, recommend those publications to the liberal patronage of the Fraternity."

To promote this laudable purpose, the Grand Lodges have recommended to the Fraternity temperance and early hours; a general observance of which, I am persuaded, would not only afford ample leisure for scientific investigations, but would also operate very favorably both for the welfare and credit of society; and it is much to be wished that such a system of discipline could be established by authority in our own Lodges; for a laxity of practice in these particulars is calculated to introduce loose and incorrect habits, which cannot fail to prove injurious to the popularity of the Order. If a Lodge be opened beyond the prescribed time, its labors may be protracted, particularly if its members are too much attached to its refreshments, to a late hour, which is inconsistent with domestic comfort, and promises to create female dissatisfaction, and perhaps hostility.

There is a delicate sensibility in the female mind which is easily excited, and an impression may be made in a moment, which will be found difficult to eradicate. The members of a Lodge therefore ought to be particularly on their guard that an unfavorable prejudice against the Craft be not created; because in such a case, every little deviation, which under extraordinary circumstances, may be unavoidable, will be magnified into a serious fault. And when transgressions, even though they be imaginary, are multiplied in the bosoms of those who ought to be most dear to every Free and Accepted Mason, and whose happiness it is their duty to promote by every attention in their power; an estrangement of heart may be occasioned, which will embitter domestic comfort, and produce misunderstandings and disagreements, for which the pleasures and enjoyments of Freemasonry will in vain be expected to compensate.

Nothing can supply the loss of domestic comfort, which is the one great source of happiness which an all-wise Creator has provided for us on earth. If, therefore, a fear of injuring the interests of Freemasonry fail to induce the observance of decorous hours in the conduct of a Lodge, let this consideration be super-added, let an attention to the comforts, and a respect for the prejudices of their families, prompt the Fraternity to avoid late sittings. It is a practice which answers no one good purpose, which secures no valuable end, which conveys no true gratification in the enjoyment, and embitters the reflections of the ensuing day. And beyond all this, it places in jeopardy those fireside comforts–those domestic virtues, which the religion we profess, the Masonry we practice, and the reason with which the divinity has endowed us–alike concur in stimulating us to cultivate and adorn.

To carry out all these points, and to bear harmless the Order during the process, much depends on the knowledge and judgment of the Master; and it is of such importance to the prosperity of Freemasonry that this officer be judiciously selected, that it behooves every candidate to consider well his capabilities for the office before his election. It is not enough that he is *au fait* at the openings and closings of the several degrees, and well acquainted with all other routine ceremonies; he ought also to be conversant with the history, the antiquity, and the philosophy of the Order;

and the tendency of its mysteries and pursuits to promote the practice of Christian morality, for on this knowledge will the success of his administration depend. In these days, bodies of men meet together for other purposes than to hear the repeated recitation of a series of common-place maxims, which soon lose their interest, and become a sounding morass and a tinkling cymbal. Even an acquaintance with the traditions of Freemasonry is not without its utility. They lead to something of a higher character, and are intimately connected with its philosophy. The most minute legend, although abstractedly it may be considered trifling and unmeaning, is not without its use, and if traced to its elements, will be found to bear a relation to facts or doctrines connected with our best and dearest interests.

It appears to me, that in the revision of the lectures at the Union, a great omission occurs which it would be well to supply, and in the present taste for scientific lectures and investigations, nothing would tend to elevate the character of Freemasonry more than to afford an opportunity for its indulgence by furnishing the means of carrying out the references of the Order, by the introduction of a higher range of science.

Freemasonry, to be completely successful, should take precedence in science, as it does in morals and the exercise of heaven-born charity; and there is no institution under the sun which equals it in the walks of benevolence. Its charities are unrivalled. It cherishes the orphan—it supports the widow—it relieves the destitute—and it provides for the worthy aged Brother an asylum from the storms of penury and indigence, at that helpless period of life when he is no longer able to wrestle with adversity.

It is true the seven liberal sciences are referred to in the second degree; but, with the exception of Geometry, they occupy no important place in a lecture. And for this reason, I suppose, that in ancient times the Order is said to have been denominated Geometry. On this science, with its application to architecture, our disquisitions are abundant and powerfully interesting; and why should not a lecture on the elementary principles of other sciences be equally gratifying to the members of a Lodge?

Arithmetic, or the science of Number, is nearly allied to Geometry; we patronize Music in practice, but hear nothing of it in theory; and of Astronomy we are merely told that 'it is an art by which we are taught to read the wonderful works of God in those sacred pages, the celestial hemisphere. While we are employed in the study of this science, we must perceive unparalleled instances of wisdom and goodness, and through the whole of the creation trace the glorious Author by his works."

It is, however, my chief intention in this paper, to offer a few desultory remarks on the science of Number; which, although the institution of Freemasonry is based upon it, has no authorized lecture to illustrate its fundamental principles, no scientific disquisitions to display its mysterious properties. At every step we take, we find a triad reference, but the reasons why this occurs are not satisfactorily explained. The monad, the duad, the triad, and the tetrad, meet us at every turn, and though these numbers constitute the foundation of all arithmetical calculations, the candidate is not fully instructed how they operate or in what manner they ought to be applied.

A large portion of the Egyptian philosophy and religion seems to have been constructed almost wholly upon the mysterious properties of numbers; and we are assured by Kircher, that everything in nature was explained on this principle alone. The Pythagoreans had so high an opinion of number, that they considered it to be the first principle of all things, and thought a knowledge of numbers to be a knowledge of God. The founder of the sect received his instructions in this science from the Egyptian priests, who taught that "the monad possesses the nature of the efficient cause, while the duad is merely a passive matter. A point corresponds with the monad, both being indivisible, and as the monad is the principle of numbers, so is the point of lines. A line corresponds with the duad, both being considered by transition. A line is length without breadth, extending between two points. A superficies corresponds with the triad, because in addition to the duad, length, it possesses a third property, viz. breadth. Again, setting down three points, two opposites, the third at the juncture of the lines made by the other two, we represent a superficies. A solid or cube represents the tetrad, for if we make three points, and set a fourth over them, we have a solid body in the form of a pyramid, which hath three dimensions, length, and breadth, and thickness."

In expressing their opinion of the Platonic bodies, the followers of Pythagoras argued that the world was made by God in thought not in time, tie commenced his work in fire and the fifth element: for there are five figures of solid bodies, which are termed mathematical. Earth was made of a cube, *fire* of a pyramid, *air* of an octaedron, *water* of an icosaedron, the sphere of the universe of a dodecaedron. And the combinations of the monad, as the principle of all things, are thus deduced. From the monad came the indeterminate duad, from them came numbers; from numbers, points; from points, lines; from lines, superfices: from superfices, solids; from these solid bodies, whose elements are four, *viz.*, fire, water, air, earth; of all of which, under various transmutations, the world consists of.

This great philosopher, Pythagoras, who, by the superiority of his mind, infused a new spirit into the science and learning of Greece, and founded the Italic sect, taught his disciples Geometry, that they might be able to deduce a reason for all their thoughts and actions, and to ascertain correctly the truth or falsehood of any proposition by the unerring process of mathematical demonstration. Thus, being enabled to contemplate the reality of things, and to detect imposture and deceit, they were pronounced to be in the road to perfect happiness. Such was the discipline and teaching of the Pythagorean Lodges. It is related, that when Justin Martyr applied to a learned Pythagorean to be admitted as a candidate for the mysterious dogmata of his philosophy, he was asked whether as a preliminary step; he had already studied the sciences of Arithmetic,

Music, Astronomy, and Geometry, which were the four divisions of the Mathematics, according to the system of Pythagoras. And he was told that it was impossible to understand the perfection of beatitude without them, because they alone are able to abstract the soul from sensibles, and to prepare it for intelligibles. He was told that, in the absence of these sciences, no man is able to contemplate what is honest, or to determine what is good. And because the candidate acknowledged his ignorance of them, he was refused admission into the society.

Above all other sciences or parts of the mathematics, however, the followers of Pythagoras esteemed the doctrine of Numbers, which they believed to have been revealed to man by the celestial deities. And they esteemed arithmetic the most ancient of all the sciences, because being naturally first generated, it takes away the rest with itself, but is not taken away with them. Thus, animal is first in nature before man; for taking away animal we take away man, but not in taking away man do we take animal. They considered the creation of the world only as the harmonious effect of a pure arrangement of number. Thus Dryden:

> *From harmony, from heavenly harmony.*
> *This universal frame began;*
> *From harmony to harmony.*
> *Through all the compass of the notes it ran.*
> *The diapason closing full in man.*

Pythagoras asserted, according to Censorinus that "the world is made according to musical proportion; and that the seven planets, which govern the nativities of mortals, have a harmonious motion, and intervals corresponding to musical diastemes, and render various sounds according to their several distances, so consonant that they make the sweetest melody, but inaudible to us by reason of the greatness of the noise, which the narrow passage of our ears is incapable of receiving."

According to the above doctrine, the monad was made to be the father of Number, and the duad its mother; whence the universal prejudice in favor of odd numbers, the father being had in greater honor than the mother. Odd numbers being masculine were considered perfect and applicable to the celestial gods, while even numbers, being female, were imperfect, and given to the terrestrial and infernal deities. Virgil has recorded several instances of this predilection in favor of odd numbers. In his eighth Eclogue he says;

Tema tibi hsc primum triplid diversa colore Licia circumd;
terque luec altaria drcum
EfSgiem duoo: Humero deoa impare gaudtt.

Thus translated by Dryden -
Around his waxen image first I wind
Three woollen fillets of three colours loin'd;
Thrice bind about his thrice devoted head.
Which round the sacred altar thrice is led.
Unequal numbers please the gods.

The eastern nations at the present day appear to reverse this principle. When two young persons are betrothed, the number of letters in each of their names is subtracted, the one from the other, and if the remainder be an even number, it is considered a favorable omen, but if it be odd, the inference is that the marriage will be unfortunate.

There are some curious superstitions still existing in our own country in favor of particular numbers. A Scottish minister, who wrote a treatise on witchcraft in 1705, says, "are there not some who cure diseases by the charm of numbers, after the example of Balaam, who used magiam geometricam?–build me here seven altars, and prepare me seven oxen and seven rams, &c. There are some witches who enjoin the sick to dip their shirt seven times in water that runs towards the south." Sir Henry Ellis has collected many instances of the use of odd numbers, in his notes on Brand's Popular Antiquities, to which the curious reader is referred.

The superstition of divination by number, called Arithmancy, was so firmly planted in the mind of man by the observances of ancient times, that it appears impossible entirely to eradicate it. An old writer quaintly remarks, on the authorities at the foot of the page; "I will not be superstitiously opinionated of the mysteries of numbers, though it be of longe standing amongst many learned men, neither will I positively affirm that the number of six is fatall to women, and the numbers of seven and nine to men, or that those numbers have (as many have written), *magnum in tota rerum natura potestatem* **(A great man the nature of the power of the whole of things)**, great power in kingdoms and common-wealth's, in families, ages, of bodies, sickness, health, wealth, losse, &c., or with Seneca and others, septimus quisque annus, &c. Each seaventh year is remarkable with men, as the sixth is with women. Or, as divines teach, that in the number of seaven there is a misticall perfection which our understandinge cannot attaine unto, and that nature herself is observant of this number."

"Masonic Offering" to the Rev. George Oliver, D.D.

MASONIC OFFERING TO THE REV. GEO. OLIVER, D.D.

The Ninth of May 1844, will stand as a red letter day in the Masonic Annals of the Ancient City of Lincoln, when the several Lodges of the Province of Lincolnshire sent their delegates to an assembly of Masons who were summoned to pay the homage of the heart to the reverend and distinguished Brother who has devoted a youth of manliness, a maturity of thought, and the dignity of age, to the service of his Church, society at large, and the Masonic fraternity to which he is attached equally by principle and by love.

The bells rung merrily and there was joy in the faces of all, the Brethren felt the moment to be a holy-day, and even the denizens of the ancient city, however they envied them the enjoyment of the day, still it was so far from an ungracious sentiment, for the occasion was welcomed by a unanimous feeling of satisfaction, that. Doctor Oliver, so well known, and so much respected by every class of society, was about to receive a public mark of Masonic gratitude.

Having in various numbers given the several accounts of the meetings, in reference to this "Masonic Offering," it is only needed here to enter into some more immediate explanation of a few material points connected with a matter of such interest and importance.

In the month of January, 1842, Dr. Crucefix addressed a letter to Bro. W. A. Nicholson, Prov. G. Sup. W. for Lincolnshire, on the propriety of presenting a Masonic Offering to Dr. Oliver, from which letter we have been permitted to select the following passage;

"On my return from Grantham, now more than two years since, where for the first time I exchanged personal relations with our justly esteemed and venerated Brother, Dr. Oliver, I seriously determined to plan, aye, and to execute (D. V.) a design which I had long contemplated, viz., that of causing to be presented to him in the name of Freemasonry, some proper tribute as an acknowledgement of his general excellence.

I only waited to see him, much subject matter of deep reflection passes through the alembic of the "mind's eye" in a few minutes' conversation, that years of correspondence, however unreserved, often fail to develop. . . During to me a most eventful period, our beloved Dr. Oliver encouraged and sustained me, and by his presence in London on the 24th of last November, he closed a series of kindnesses, but only to renew them with added fervor. I allude to these particulars, to shew that intensely affected as my spirits have been, they could not earlier permit me to enter on the desirable project I am aware that the Witham Lodge has paid our friend a compliment, but I am morally assured that an expression of the universal esteem in which he is held by the world of Masons will be regarded by him with feelings of justifiable pride; he cannot be unconscious of his own exalted merit. Lincolnshire, his homestead, should lead, London should adopt and the world should confirm the testimony of our order to its most distinguished member, by the purest wreath that should grace the brow of the Freemason of all time There should be a Provincial Committee in Lincoln to co-operate with a London Committee, and all foreign and district Grand Lodges should be addressed.

"The presentation can take place at the Provincial Grand Lodge at Lincoln in the summer of 1843."

Brother Nicholson's reply was couched in the most affectionate acknowledgement of Dr. Oliver's worth, but regretted that his own indisposition and the still severer affliction of Mrs. Nicholson would prevent him from taking an active part in so important an object.

Bro. Sir Ed. Bromhead was consulted; and here again, a serious obstacle presented itself. Sir Edward was afflicted with so serious an affection in the eyes as to preclude him also from taking the lead. At length, a Central Committee was formed at Lincoln, with whom the London Brethren put themselves into immediate communication. The Chairman of the Central Committee, Bro. Hebb, (Mayor of Lincoln,) died during last year, and sometime elapsed before the appointment of his successor the Rev. J. O. Dakeyne. Much delay, having thus of necessity occurred, some further time was required to address the fraternity in the East and West Indies, and other distant places. The result, however, has been a triumphant testimony of the love, gratitude, and veneration felt for the distinguished Dr. Oliver, which, however, exhibited in the complimentary offering, derives a higher value from the correspondence that has flowed in from Brethren of social rank and Masonic influence in all parts of the world. We have seen letters which, if published, would form a volume of a most interesting character.

It is important for reasons of obvious delicacy, that the attention of our readers should be drawn to the date of the first suggestion of the offering, which was in January 1842, now more than two years since; next, that the delay was accidental; and thirdly, that until the subscriptions should be remitted from the distant hemisphere, the "Offering" itself could not have been commenced.

THE PRESENTATION CUP.
ACCOMPANYING THE MASONIC OFFERING TO THE
REVD. GEO. OLIVER, D.D.
MAY. 9TH 1844.

Author and Managing Eitor
Darrell Jordan

Darrell Jordan is an acolyte of the August Fraternity, former Noble Grand-IOOF and Freemason. He is also a member of the Theosophical and Philalethes Societies.

About the Managing Editor

Darrell Jordan is an acolyte of the August Fraternity, former Noble Grand-IOOF and Freemason. He is also a member of the Theosophical and Philalethes Societies.

Darrell Jordan

Manly P. Hall - All Seeing Eye Book Series

Manly P. Hall - A Seeker of More Intelligent Life Book

Books By The Managing Editor

Exoteric Christianity

The Initiates Speak

Arthur Edward Waite, Forgotten Essays

For More Information about books, please visit:
Parallel47North.com/collections/esoteric-books
Info@Parallel47North.com

Artist and Illustrator
Jessica Naomi

Hand-drawn illustrations and portraits.
The artist portfolio:
JessicaNaomiDesigns.com

Hand-Drawn Portrait of George Oliver

Manly P. Hall

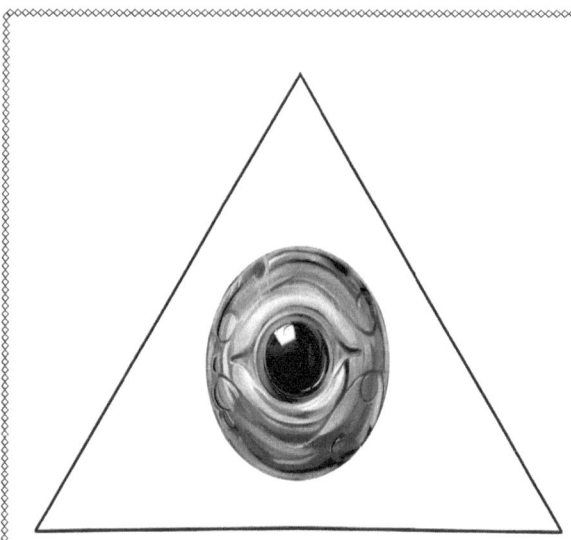

All Seeing Eye

Other Illustrations & Portraits by the Artist

Hiram E. Butler

Arthur Edward Waite

www.ingramcontent.com/pod-product-compliance
Lightning Source LLC
Chambersburg PA
CBHW020310010526
44107CB00001B/54